# What People are Saying About Drunk with Wonder

*Drunk With Wonder* is where *Conversations with God* meets *What the Bleep Do we Know?*

*Scott. R., Chair*
*Orange County, CA CODA*

*Drunk with Wonder* is a book that can untangle and reweave your life. Make no mistake – if you read this book, you can never go back to being a victim, a loser or a couch potato helplessly watching the movie of your life. You will come into a never-before-imagined power and finally learn what it means to Grow Up.

*Barbara Gardner, PhD*
*Author of The Sai Prophecy (HCI)*

"As a New Thought Minister, I am constantly on the search for speakers and books that clearly present the Truth Principles, the Universal Laws under which the Spiritual Universe operates. This book does just that, in an easy to read format, engaging your attention while it gently and inexorably leads the reader back to a path of accessing the Wisdom Within. If put into practice, the Truth Principles outlined here will set one free."

*Reverend Tanya Wyldflower*
*Mendocino Religious Science Center*
*for Spiritual Awakening*

I so enjoyed your "message to the masses." It is very enlightening and has awakened in me a new level of understanding that I hope to be able to put to use. It also has helped to reinforce some of my own beliefs in the human race and how it can heal itself.

I'm glad you shared your higher self's wisdom, and if only 1% of the world could read and put to practice these great words to live by, then you will have done the world a great service.

*Namaste,*
*Gary Watson, retired designer*

# Drunk with Wonder

*Awakening to the God Within*

MAY ALL YOUR DREAMS MANIFEST EFFORTLESSLY BEFORE YOU ARE EVEN AWARE OF THEM.

**Steve Ryals**

Published by
Rock Creek Press
PO Box 789, Ukiah, CA 95482 USA
www.rockcreekpress.com



Printed in the United States of America by McNaughton & Gunn
Book design: Steven D. Ryals, with grateful and heartfelt acknowledgement to David Smith at NineTrees Design
Cover design: Calvin Turnwall of Real Smart Art
Index: Medea Minnich, medea@mcn.org
Printed with soy-based ink
Paper: 60# Thor Offset acid-free, recycled paper - please recycle!

Publisher's Cataloging-in-Publication
(Provided by Quality Books, Inc.)

Ryals, Steve.
Drunk with wonder : awakening to the God within / by Steve Ryals. -- 1st ed.
p. cm.

1. Spiritual life. 2. Success. 3. Spirituality. 4. Conduct of life. I. Title.

BL624.R93 2006 204'.4
QBI06-700050

ISBN 1-933906-17-0

10 9 8 7 6 5 4 3 2

# Dedication

I dedicate this book to my dear friend, Franklin Markowitz, who spent hundreds and hundreds of hours giving me his eagle-eyed editing and wise counsel. Your clarity and strength of vision permeate virtually every page. Thanks to your tireless efforts and your gentle coaching on using conscious language, this book has turned into something magical. My gratitude is boundless, my thanks a never-ending shower of love.

I also dedicate this book to my Beloved, JoAnn SkyWatcher, and to my family and friends. Your love, patience and incredible support are ample evidence of miracles on Earth. I also want to acknowledge the immense help of the Challenge Day community, particularly the founders, Yvonne and Rich Dutra-St John.

To Garvin Deshazer, who helped erect the skeleton and hugely supported me in the early stages.

To my sister Quana. You believed in my higher self long before I did.

To Marilyn Gordon. Without your help, my higher self may never have begun to speak. I still have all those early tapes!

And to Robert Frey, a dear friend and trusted mentor. I miss you.

I wish to extend my undying gratitude for the people who read the manuscript and offered a multitude of cogent and helpful suggestions: Kim Kakade, Christina Turnwall, Quana Ryals, Doug Waagen, Barbara Ryals (Mom), Scott Ryals, Eileen Peterson, Stacey Sheldon, Rev. Tanya Wyldflower, Barbara Gardner and Shirley Freriks. My heart overflows with gratitude!

Finally, to my father, Stanley Ryals. While we had some challenging times, in the end our love for each other won out. Thank you, Dad, for your unwavering love. I wish I could share this book with you. I think you would be very proud.

# Contents

# I Introduction

> Someday, after mastering the winds, the waves, the tides and gravity, we shall harness the energy of love, and then, for the second time in the history of the world, man will discover fire.
>
> – *Teilhard de Chardin*

My shooting buddy Richard expertly speared my flesh. After a well-practiced ballet of pulling the plunger back and loosening the rubber hose around my upper arm, blood spurted up into the solution of water and pure crystal methedrine. Then, with a gentle push on the plunger, Richard flushed the mix of blood and drugs into my body.

As the rush built I began to gasp, knowing I had only seconds to lurch into a standing position and stumble into my room. I fell onto the unmade bed, indifferent to the peeling wallpaper and a grimy window that framed the ruined yard. I noticed my unattended cigarette burning in the ashtray, smoke curling lazily into the thick air. As much as I wanted a drag, I couldn't muster the strength to reach for it.

As the speed pulsed through my veins, my vision narrowed as if I had slipped into a tunnel. My heart thundered in my ears, easily beating 200 times a minute, and every cell in my body began screaming in rough ecstasy.

A calm, gentle voice spoke into the chaos of my senses. "So, did you get enough this time?" I feebly craned my neck to see who was speaking, but I was alone. Then I realized that this must be the same inner voice who had been speaking more and more lately, especially when I was peaking on LSD or over-amped on meth.

“What’s it to you?” My thoughts seemed dull, uncaring. “Maybe I’ll die this time, and you can go bother someone else, someone who gives a damn.” The voice fell silent, and my body shuddered as the effects of the speed reached their peak.

“Holy shit,” a familiar voice boomed through the fog. “It stinks in here!” I groaned inwardly. Damn it all, that stupid, nagging voice is back. What was I going to have to do to get it to shut up?

“Steve! Hey man, are you OK?”

With a supreme effort, I peeled my eyes open to see an indistinct figure looming over me. Slowly, like a cartoon running at half speed, Carl’s face fluttered into place. Carl had been one of my best friends for the past couple of years, but since I had fallen into the rabbit hole of shooting speed I hadn’t seen much of him.

“You look terrible!” His face reddened with each word. “What the hell are you doing to yourself?” Carl’s voice, all jagged edges and razor wire, cut little notches through the speed, and I vaguely remembered something about him coming out for a visit. His disgust made me feel like scuttling off into a black hole. Incandescent shame seared my soul as I tasted myself through his eyes.

Without warning, strong hands gripped my face and forced my mouth open. A familiar pill crawled down my throat. “OK, Steve, you always loved acid. Here’s an eight-way purple Owsley. It’ll either kill you or cure you. Right now, I don’t much care which.” With that, Carl stomped out of my room and slammed the door. His raging contempt felt like hot pokers blistering my heart.

He doesn’t care either, I thought as my eyelids sagged. No one cares. Dimly, I realized how maudlin that sounded, self-disgust welling up like tears. I managed a weak snort. Even I don’t give a rat shit, I concluded, allowing the speed to carry me away. I'd already forgotten about Carl and the LSD. "I care."

That voice again! I began mulling over ways to shut it up for good, but before I got very far the acid, enthusiastically helped along by the speed, tore like a tornado through my awareness. My consciousness, such as it was, began drifting out of my body, eventually bumping along the ceiling like a helium balloon. This is a trip, I thought with a giggle. I'm having an out-of-body experience. I wondered if this meant I was about to die, and I realized that I couldn't find any place in me that seemed to care.

"Look at yourself," the quiet, calm voice suggested. Indifferently, I rolled the balloon of my consciousness over so I could look down. Shock shuddered through me like an earthquake. Could that really be me? Emaciated, grubby, smelly, pale as a moonlit night, I wondered through a growing sense of panic if I was already dead.

"Not quite," the voice replied, as if on cue. "But if you shoot that much speed again any time soon, you will be."

Staring down at my limp body, breath shallow, heart racing, I realized the voice was right. I had been trying to kill myself for months, and here was my chance. One more hit would do it. At that moment, staring over the abyss, I realized I had a choice. Live, or die?

This all happened a long time ago, in April of 1968. Obviously, I chose life, at least of a sort. As soon as I came down, I called my parents and asked to come home. Only 18 at the time, I never shot speed, or anything else, again. Three weeks later, on May 1, Carl died in a motorcycle accident, the victim of a drunk driver. I said for years that Carl saved my life, but what he really did was give me an opportunity to see that I had a choice. And choice is what this book, *Drunk with Wonder: Awakening to the God Within*, is all about.

It's been 15 years since my higher self again made its presence known to me. It was only then that I could begin fully to appreciate Sir Eddington's famous comment, "Not only is the universe stranger than we imagine, it is stranger than we *can* imagine."

My name is Steve Ryals, and this book is about how I awakened to my Divinity, and about how you can awaken to your Divinity as well. I've spent a lifetime developing and honing this material, as well as integrating my headstrong inner child with the vast wisdom of my higher self. I am both honored and humbled to have the opportunity to share this perspective with you.

*Drunk with Wonder* looks at science, spirituality, intentionality and the importance of transformative practices in creating the world of our dreams. We see the apparently disparate realms of science and spirituality as two sides of the same coin. Using tools available in each of these realms, we will actually pick up the "coin" of reality and examine it from a fresh perspective. We will also take a close look at discernment, which we define as, "the act or process of exhibiting keen insight and good judgment"; and intuition, which is "the act or faculty of knowing or sensing without the use of rational processes, or immediate cognition."

You will find numerous transformative practices throughout the book. When used consistently, these processes will expand and enhance your ability to experience the present moment with joy and serenity, ecstasy and stillness, passionately alive yet unattached to the outcome. You will see that paradox lies at the heart of all experience, and we will thoroughly explore the fascinating dance of life as we journey together on an inner voyage of discovery.

Please understand from the outset that you are Divinity personified. If you happen to be skeptical about the idea that you are indeed Divine, this material may make you uncomfortable, at least at first. I ask that you suspend judgment for now. I will clearly define what I mean by

Divinity early on, and trust that your higher self will respond in a way that works for you. As I will remind you throughout the book, you cannot do this awakening wrong. After all, you are God in form!

*Drunk with Wonder* also explores the idea that God manifests throughout all of creation, from galactic clusters to amoeba, from black holes to a brilliant sunrise. For now, just consider the possibility that God does not make mistakes – ever! You are not merely a reflection of God, but literally God made manifest.

Before we get into the book, I want to share with you some details about my life. I was born in 1949, and grew up in the placid 50s and wild 60s. In many ways, I was an archetypal child of that time, raised in accordance with the conventional standards of that era. Though my parents loved me and did the best they could raising my four younger brothers and me, the truth is they had their own issues, which they unintentionally passed on to us.

For me, childhood was filled with feelings of profound loneliness and unworthiness. I soon came to accept the belief that I was not enough, and could never measure up to my father's seemingly impossible standards. By 1967, I had run away from home and was living in a crash pad in the Haight-Ashbury district of San Francisco. I did everything I could to hide from my insecurities in a world filled with sex, drugs, and rock n' roll. It was the "Summer of Love," and though I claimed that banner for myself, paradoxically I often felt lost in suicidal despair.

Years later, after many adventures as well as traumatic losses, I decided something had to change. While still a hippie at heart, I resolved that, in the interest of self-preservation, I would attempt to conform to my parent's (and society's) expectations. I got a degree, got married, then divorced, got a haircut, then a job, got married again, started businesses, made money, lost money and got divorced again. In addition, I continually did my best to keep from feeling anything by submerging myself in alcohol, drugs, TV and always staying busy. Sound familiar?

Over time, I realized that in spite of my best attempts to stay numb, I had spent most of my life desperately seeking answers to questions that terrified me. Questions such as, "Why do I feel so separate and alone? Why don't I ever feel as though I'm enough? What's the meaning of my life? Why am I even here?" And perhaps the most puzzling questions of all: "What is life all about? What's the point?"

In the absence of answers, I became a master at avoiding the questions. Whenever I dared to consider one of them, all I found was pain and confusion. Over and over again, in my futile efforts to avoid these questions and the scary feelings they engendered, I nearly destroyed myself. Shortly after Carl's death, I started using alcohol, and soon learned about its amazing power to numb the soul. Alcohol soon became my favorite substance to abuse, and I battled it, mostly unsuccessfully, for the next 33 years.

This cycle of pain and self-abuse finally began to change when I became reacquainted with my higher self.

In 1991 I paid a visit to Marilyn Gordon,[1] a friend and hypnotherapist I trusted. I thought that she might be able to help me understand an amazing dream I'd recently had. As Marilyn brought me into a hypnotic trance for the first time, she felt prompted to ask a question that had nothing to do with my ostensible reason for being there. She asked whether there was anyone who wanted to speak. A wise, calm voice immediately replied, saying simply, "Why, I'm your higher self. Who did you think it would be?" It turned out to be the same voice that had spoken to me all those years ago during the chaos of my drug abuse.

Marilyn and my higher self proceeded to have the first of many conversations, which eventually ranged from the nature of the self to the nature of reality. Being in a deep hypnotic state at the time, I had no idea that this exchange was happening. When I came out of the trance Marilyn played the cassette of the session back to me. I was dumbfounded, to say the least, and more than a little frightened. It took some time before it began to sink in that my life was about to irrevocably change.

There were many more of these sessions over the next several months. In one of them, my higher self said that I was his eyes and ears in this life; the vehicle, as he affectionately calls me, through which he would share his gentle wisdom with the world. Years went by before I finally began to understand the larger truth that my higher self is nothing less than who I really am, and ultimately a reflection of who we *all* really are. I've spent the past 15 years integrating with my higher self, and *Drunk with Wonder* is our gift to the world.

With my higher self's endlessly patient help, I have learned to see the light of Divine Presence shining in the eyes of every living being. I have come to realize that who we really are is the moment-by-moment manifestation of this light.

It's become quite clear that many of us, including myself, spend most of our lives lost in "Fear-Based-Consciousness," agonizing over the past and worrying about the future. Is it really any wonder, then, that we feel emotionally and physically exhausted so much of the time?

Becoming familiar with my higher self's great wisdom and profound truth has completely changed my life. After decades of alcohol and drug abuse, I am now sober, and I am pleased to say that I routinely experience a level of peace and serenity that for many years I would not have believed possible. I do not mean to imply that I have transcended my humanity, but rather that I have embraced it.

Though from time to time I still deal with my deepest stories of not being good enough (along with the panoply of intense emotions they engender), on a day-to-day basis my life is filled with passion, purpose and play. I know that I'm making a difference in the world, and that's what matters most. It's not just my dream, but my unshakable conviction, that making a positive contribution to the world we leave for our children and grandchildren is absolutley vital. It is only by our coming together as a global community that we will create a world where every child, and indeed every one of us, feels safe, loved and celebrated.

Many people have asked me what it feels like to embrace my higher self. Being as real as I can be in this moment, I will say that sometimes it's a mixed bag. While the experience itself is filled with calm euphoria and numinous peace, many times I thought I was going off the deep end, and that the folks in the white coats were going to burst in at any moment and take me away. It has taken a long time for me to fully own that I am as worthy as any other to experience my higher self. One of my goals in writing this book is to make it just a little easier for others to be able to embrace their higher selves than it was for me.

And so it goes. Please understand that, at one time or another, I have struggled with virtually all of the subjects we discuss in this book. As the years have gone by, I've come to trust this inner wisdom. While my higher self never makes me wrong for my choices, if I specifically ask, he will cheerfully point out consequences and perspectives I hadn't thought of. As he repeatedly says, "The greatest gift we could possibly give you would be to reflect the truth of who you really are, which is nothing less than God incarnate." Or, as Valentine Michael Smith famously stated in Robert Heinlein's *Stranger in a Strange Land*, "Thou art God."

It's my fervent hope that, as you get to know "us" through the pages of this book, you will open to the Divine Presence of your higher self. While you may or may not experience that presence as a distinct voice, I know that simply by moving your own thoughts to the side and inviting the omnipresent light to shine through you, new and amazing possibilities will become manifest.

I want to emphasize that my higher self speaks mostly in the plural, using the terms we, or us. It also uses pronouns such as him and her interchangeably, teaching that at the core of our individuality lies One Heart, One Spirit, and that this Spirit is not gender-based.

Numerous terms, including Spirit, Creator, God, God/Goddess and Divine Presence, are tantamount to the same essential truth, that the Great Mystery contains within Itself all those concepts and much, much more. The deepest truth, which I will repeat often in this book, is that there is only One of Us here, only One Heart, of which we are all infinitely precious sparks.

One note on formatting: the questions in *italics* represent life stages I went through earlier, while the terms we, us and our represent my integrated higher self. I created many of these questions by looking through my journals, so please understand that they are my attempt to reflect my initial reactions when I first confronted these questions.

As you read, I suggest that you write down any questions you may have. If they remain unanswered through the course of the book, you may submit them to me at *questions@drunkwithwonder.com*. I do ask that you hold off on emailing questions until you are finished with the book, as I'm going to cover a lot of ground and answers may arise during our time together. You see, one of the purposes of this book is to help you learn how to listen, *really* listen, to the still, small voice inside of you. This voice awaits your attention. It holds the highest wisdom to every question in your life. Here, always available in your heart, lies the sweet mystery of your very own higher self.

Some final notes: where applicable, I have included relevant notes for those of you who are so inclined to explore these subjects in greater depth. Please turn to the back of the book for an extensive bibliography, recommended reading list, a list of publications with which I stay current as well as additional resources.

The poetry, all of which I have written over the past 15 years, is meant to illustrate various feelings I've had during this journey.

And now, I warmly welcome you to *Drunk with Wonder*.

# Drunk with Wonder

# 1 The Nature of Knowing

> There is one spectacle grander than the sea, that is the sky; there is one spectacle grander than the sky, that is the interior of the soul.
>
> – *Victor Hugo*

Namaste, hello and, once again, welcome. Namaste is Sanskrit for "The God in me honors the God in you."

I have journaled extensively over the years, and the dialogue format of this book reflects some of the conversations I have had with my higher self. Simply think of the questions as coming from a younger, more fear-based me, and the responses from that higher place deep within us all.

I don't claim to have any answers for you. Once you've learned how to access your higher self, you'll discover that all the answers you will ever need have always been available to you. When you come to fully appreciate this, you will find all your questions answered from within. Please trust that you will recognize when your inner voice is offering guidance for your highest good. Now, let's begin by creating some context.

*OK. Why don't you talk a bit about who or what you are.*

To put it as simply as possible, we are a manifestation of All-That-Is, the animating spark of consciousness that you might think of as your soul, or higher self.

*Wow, that seems like quite an ostentatious claim!*

It is neither ostentatious nor a claim. It is simply a fact. We are a Divine expression of All-That-Is, and so are you.

*What do you mean, so am I?*

Every single human being is a deeply cherished manifestation of All-That-Is. Like all people, and all of creation for that matter, Divinity is your birthright. Every thing (by which we mean all facets of the universe), whether or not you consider it alive, is also an expression of the infinitely loving heart of All-That-Is. For thousands of years, numerous spiritual traditions have taught that there is really no separation between us. In *Drunk with Wonder,* we heartily affirm that teaching.

Recent scientific discoveries bear this out. For the sake of making sure our readers are on the same page, let's review some basic material. For those who are already familiar with this information, please bear with us. Throughout the course of *Drunk with Wonder*, we'll be looking at how the seemingly disparate teachings of science and spirituality are actually describing the same phenomenon, albeit from what appear to be radically different perspectives.

For example, perhaps you've heard that some cosmologists consider the universe to be holographic. A hologram is a three-dimensional image contained within a photosensitive medium, such as a flat glass plate. The most amazing quality of a hologram is that, if the plate is broken, no matter into how many fragments, each fragment still contains the entire image.

*I've known about holograms for years, but I still find it a difficult concept to grasp.*

Quite understandable, though it's not really an issue here. When we call the universe holographic, we simply mean that each part, no matter how infinitesimal it may appear, contains the essence of the entire universe. Similarly, every cell in your body contains the DNA blueprint for your entire body, everything from your skin color to how long your eyelashes are. This underlying holographic truth is also the source of the foundational belief of many spiritual traditions, including Buddhism, Hinduism, Sufism and many indigenous cultures.

*I was raised in the Unitarian Church. Sunday school largely consisted of increasingly detailed studies of comparative religion, so I have at least a little familiarity with those traditions.*

That's a great place to start. If you're willing to explore the concept of Unity Consciousness (which both the Unitarian and Unity churches have explicitly used in their names), you will find it to be at the core of almost all theology. Jesus said, "Lift up a stone and you will find me there; split a piece of wood and I am there." Experiments in quantum physics have repeatedly validated this ancient wisdom.

More recently, superstring theories appear able to unify (at least mathematically), the four measurable forces in the universe (electromagnetic, gravity, weak and strong nuclear forces), in a way that eluded Einstein. The latest work in this field unifies five different string theory models into what is being called M-theory.[2] This grand theory, which currently exhibits no known mathematical defects, is the closest we've come so far towards scientifically describing the underlying unity of the universe.

Physicists have also demonstrated that every subatomic particle is fundamentally connected, and that no particle can exist without affecting other particles, as well as being affected by them. Recent experiments with quantum entanglement show conclusively that this connection is not bound by space or time. As with many of the ideas we'll mention in this book, there is a plethora of information readily available in books or on the Internet.

Taking this idea of an underlying connection between the four measurable forces of the universe a step farther, it's crucial to understand that every observation we make affects what we observe. A clear example of this idea is the classic double-slit experiment.[3] One version concludes that light is composed of particles of energy called photons. With a simple variation in this experiment, observing that same beam of light shows just as conclusively that it is a wave, or frequency, and not composed of particles at all.

The deeper truth, which can be most disconcerting, is that light is simultaneously composed of both particles *and* waves. It's the way we look at light that determines whether we observe a particle or a wave. In other words, the universe and our experience of it are inextricably linked. The essence of human experience is filled with paradox, something mystics of all traditions have intuitively known.

*That's a lot to take in. I'm not sure where you're going with this.*

Please bear with us for a moment. Where we are going is that, while science has become adept at describing the physical universe, there are innumerable observable phenomena that have so far defied conventional understanding. Science has learned to describe physical reality quite well, as far as it goes. Space, time, energy and matter have had volumes written about their empirical qualities. Simply referring to the physical attributes of something, however, particularly a living, breathing being, or quantifying the forces acting upon it, fails to capture its essence, or Spirit.

Over the past several thousand years, countless experiential observations have been made for which there have been no corresponding physical data. These experiential observations form the core of metaphysics. One of the main goals of *Drunk with Wonder* is to bridge the apparent gap between physics and metaphysics. By the end of the book, our hope is that you will appreciate that these two apparently disparate disciplines actually describe different aspects of the same universe within which we find ourselves.

This underlying, unifying Spirit, or Divine Presence, is the thread weaving together all that exists. Spirit is unbreakable, inseparable and utterly unified, which is why we often refer to it as The One. Though most people possess preconceived notions about what Spirit is, we use this term in a way that may be new to you.

As simply as we can put it, just as breath animates the body, Spirit is the animating force of the universe. At times called the ocean of joy, or the field of pure potential, or the alpha and the omega, Spirit is the infinite Being out of which all things become manifest. As the Bible teaches, God is the great "I Am," the unbounded awareness of pure being.

One of the most basic choices you can make in your apprehension of the world is whether the universe is Divinely inspired or merely random. From our perspective, those who speak of "intelligent design" are on the right track. Where our teachings part ways with creationists centers on the idea of an angry, vengeful God sitting in judgment over the born sinners of humanity.

As you may already have gathered, our enthusiastic choice is that God is all there is, the source of an unlimited supply of life and love. From this perspective, of course the universe is not random. It has obviously been designed as a platform within which life, in its infinite glory, can flourish. However, in a way that those on the far right would no doubt find heretical, we teach that the overwhelming scientific evidence of evolution is also true.

For us, there is no contradiction between intelligent design and evolution. God did indeed create the universe, *including the laws of physics and biology*. These laws make evolution, including the evolution of life on Earth as well as countless other planets, inevitable. The infinite creative spark of the Divine takes it from the moment the universe began (In the Bible, God commanded, "Let there be light, and there was light, and it was good") to right here, right now.

With all due respect for those with differing beliefs (such as that God is judgmental, capable of anger, or reserves love for those who adhere to one, and only one, set of beliefs), we teach that God is pure, unconditional love, and that God's infinite, unending gift of love is life itself. The New Testament states this clearly, "God is Love."

The entire universe is therefore an outward manifestation, of life, the ultimate gift of love. You get to choose, on a moment-to-moment basis, what you do with this gift. Do you choose love or fear? Do you choose to own your Divinity and create the life of your dreams, or stay small and play the role of victim? In each moment, with each breath, it is your choice.

# Open or Closed

When I'm feeling expanded and awake
Shining with a starry residue
That clings provocatively
To my naked skin,

The love that flows
So freely through me
Laps tenderly at the heart
Of each Beloved

When I'm feeling closed down, asleep
Dark with worry,
Perspective forgotten
Covered with itchy old flannel

The love I am
Lies immersed in
An icy pool
Under the blazing night

In my favorite dream I'm centered,
Balanced Gracefully
Between big and small,
Breathing, Being

In my worst nightmare
I've forgotten how to expand,
Contracting inexorably into
A pinpoint of darkness screaming

Dare I sleep?
Dare I dream?
Dare I not?
It's all God –

# 2 THE NATURE OF THE HIGHER SELF

The world is but a canvas to the imagination.
– *Henry David Thoreau*

*OK. While this is all fascinating, perhaps even provocative, right now I just want to come back to my first question, "Who are you?"*

Fair enough. Simply put, we are the voice of your higher self, a direct connection to your own Divinity.

*I'm not Divine, I'm a deeply flawed human being. I've had numerous addictions, and other bad habits. Sometimes I'm rude and angry for no good reason. I've often felt so sad and lonely I just wanted to die. When I was a teenager, I actually attempted suicide. How could anyone as messed up as I am ever be a home for the Divine?*

Dear one, you are not merely a home for the Divine, you are Divinity incarnate! As you will discover during our journey through this book, God set up this marvelous, absolutely compelling Passion Play so that you could experience the miracle of life from every conceivable perspective.

The nature of your higher self (modestly played by yours truly) is exactly, precisely the same as the nature of everyone's higher self; pure, unconditional love dancing with profound wisdom. As Jesus said, "The kingdom of God is within you." This was his culture's way of expressing the perennial Truth that Divinity lies within. The Biblical "Holy Spirit" is another way of of teaching that God is not separate from you. In the Jewish tradition, this Holy Spirit is called Shekina, and is considered to be the Divine Feminine. Our point is simply that the wisdom teaching that God is to be found within dates back many thousands of years.

*Then why, after all this time, doesn't everyone live from this place?*

Ah, that is the eternal question. We will be spending much of this book exploring why many people so assiduously avoid owning who they really are. For now, please let it be enough to say that who we are is a perfectly mirrored manifestation of who you are. In essence, we are who you will be when you grow up. And now, let us continue presenting our hope-filled vision for the future of this planet.

*Really? What hope? If you ask me, you have to be certifiable or incredibly courageous to see the craziness in our world and still see room for hope.*

Certifiable or courageous? An intriguing choice. How about certifiably courageous? Please allow us to continue explaining who we are, then we will begin the process of exploring the roots of our hope. As we mentioned, we are your own higher self. And what, you may well be asking, is the higher self composed of? Why, love, of course. Pure, unconditional love. Huge, vast oceans of love. Endless, delicious, infinitely fulfilling love. We embody the Source Love of the genderless God, for that is who we all truly are.

Everyone, including you, although you may sometimes deny it, is a perfectly created holographic representation of God. We are here to share the love we are with the love you are. In Christian theology, this idea is stated as,"We are created in the image and likeness of God." Or as Hafiz, the great Sufi master and poet, wrote, "Your heart and my heart are very, very old friends." Indeed, the Divine truth is simply that this entire universe is an infinitely exquisite expression of love. It's just that many of you have forgotten.

Though many wisdom traditions teach some version of this "great forgetting," one of the truths we are excited to share is that this apparent amnesia has never been a mistake or a descent into sin. As we hope you will come to see during the course of the book, it is actually an essential component of this playground of life. When you remember and fully embody this wisdom, it will feel like you've just won the ultimate game of hide and seek, for you will have rediscovered your true essence.

*For me to accept what you've been saying, I would have to believe in what I consider to be superstitious nonsense and, quite frankly, I don't. In fact, I'm not even sure I believe in God. So, where does that leave us in this dialogue?*

Actually, you do not have to believe in God. In fact, you don't *have* to believe in anything at all. What you *choose* to believe is completely up to you. For us to be in dialogue, all we need is honesty within ourselves as well as between us. Our desire is for you to see clearly that any point of disagreement is most likely where the greatest potential for growth exists. If you are truly committed to creating valuable experiences for yourself, we encourage you to keep an open mind and be willing to take a good look at what comes up. Embracing your true nature may not always be easy, but it is certainly exhilarating!

*What is my alternative, then, if you say I am a Divine being, and I don't believe in God?*

As often happens with any form of communication, what you hear may be different from what we say. It may simply be a case of semantics. You have likely read or heard several definitions of the term Divinity, which may differ from the definition we use. To agree upon any definition, we must first be in alignment with the concepts supporting it. We will take a look at those concepts next.

Drunk with Wonder

## God in Form

I Am God in form
As massive black oak
Roots, bark, branches, leaves
Connecting Mother Earth
And Father Sky
Caressing sun-warmed air
And moon-cooled breezes
Sheltering all who
Find themselves here –

Drunk with Wonder

# 3 The Dance of Intuition
# Another way of Knowing

> Intuition becomes increasingly valuable in the new information society precisely because there is so much data.
>
> – *John Naisbitt*

So, you say that you don't believe in God. Let's find out what you do believe, and more importantly, *why* you believe it. Do you accept the things you can see, hear, smell, taste or touch?

*Yes, generally, although I know my senses can be manipulated, as in the case of optical illusions.*

Excellent! Then let us begin with the senses, where we share common ground. Do you accept the validity of the scientific method, whereby observations are made, hypotheses are formed, and experiments are designed and conducted, then repeated, until theories and occasionally laws are finally developed?

*Yes, I would have to say I do, since science appears to be doing a pretty good job of revealing how the universe works, then creating new technologies based on this knowledge.*

So it's clear that the scientific method is useful in describing and understanding how various realms, including those far beyond the abilities of the five senses to apprehend, are still essential components of the universe. The unseen world revealed by electron and scanning tunneling microscopes, quantum physics, genetics, and contemporary theories of cosmology are but a few examples.

On the other end of the spectrum, for well over a decade now the Hubble Space Telescope has been providing quite astonishing pictures of our universe, producing images of galaxies and nebulas located billions of light years from Earth (which is the same as saying that we are looking billions of years into the past).

While we can't see any of these splendors with the naked eye, there is wide agreement that those galaxies exist. Or, at the very least, that these galaxies existed when the photons now striking our telescopes left their respective galaxies. Do you agree that properly calibrated instruments can give us accurate information, even though we cannot independently verify that information without the use of sophisticated hardware and computer algorithms?

*Sure, I'm with you. You're talking about computers, telescopes, microscopes, ultrasound, magnetic resonance imaging, even something as seemingly prosaic as electricity, right?*

Exactly! Now, do you believe science is complete, that we have already made all the big discoveries? Is the only thing left just to flesh out existing theories, or do you see science as a continuing process, with many layers yet to be uncovered?

*I think it would be foolish, even arrogant, for any generation to decide it had discovered all there was to know. Though we know more about some things than others, I certainly see that there still is a tremendous amount to learn.*

Excellent. It sounds as though you are willing to consider the possibility that there may be whole fields of science in which further research could lead to fascinating new discoveries. Perhaps you could name a few?

*It seems to me we could do a lot more with renewable forms of energy, farming without toxic chemicals, cures for cancer, Alzheimer's and AIDS, perhaps even life-extension. I know that in the past, as fresh theories and tools were developed, new methods of scientific inquiry became available, and so major new discoveries become likely, even inevitable. Sometimes it seems as though anything is possible.*

Given that new discoveries do indeed seem inevitable, can you imagine that many of the questions currently seen as falling within the realm of the non-scientific, such as philosophy, religion, or even metaphysics, may someday be legitimate topics for scientific investigation? The Institute of Noetic Sciences, for example, has conducted fascinating and provocative work in these areas.

*Yes, I suppose so.*

Great, then this gives us a starting point. From here, we can explore the nature of reality, the concept of time, and the essence of the universe. With this understanding, we may even be able to discuss the concept of reincarnation, possibilities as to the purpose of life, and ultimately God-As-Us.

*Whoa! How did you get all of that out of a brief discussion of science and sensory perception?*

By acknowledging that there are many things you do not yet understand, and many questions science itself has not answered, you open a space for a different kind of exploration. This journey of discovery is based on three components: your physical senses, reasonably current scientific knowledge and the unerring truth of your heart. Using these components, we will examine an expanded set of possibilities which, if you are able to accept even theoretically, will allow you to re-learn how to use your natural discernment.

*What do you mean by discernment, and how can I re-learn something I don't remember knowing in the first place?*

Discernment is a tool. You don't remember learning how to use discernment because you were born with it. You use it to distinguish light from dark, resonance from discord, balance from imbalance, that point where your knowledge and instincts intersect. You take all the information you have about a given topic, add to that everything you can learn from available sources, then filter it through your logical mind, doing your best to avoid bias or judgment. While you may not always be aware of this process, you use it on a daily basis to create every moment of your experience.

What we are suggesting here is that as you become fully conscious of this process of discernment, you can then use this awareness to more deeply appreciate your magnificence. We assure you that making choices based on your sacred essence will lead to more loving behavior.

*I'm not clear as to how discernment is tied to magnificence, though in general I guess I'm more familiar with this process than I thought. It just never occurred to me to use it to decipher ideas that seem obscure.*

Discernment is not only your birthright, it is an inextricable part of your Divinity. You were born with a finely tuned sense of natural knowing, or instinctual awareness, honed over millions of years of evolution. Instincts allowed you to suckle, to swallow, and to cry for help. Your instincts served you well then, or you wouldn't be here now.

However, your natural knowing, what we call discernment, soon bumps up against your experiences of living in the world. One example would be, when you were an infant, feeling hungry at an inconvenient time for your caregiver to feed you. Under such circumstances, it wouldn't take long to begin discounting your discernment and creating stories to explain, justify or rationalize this discontinuity.

Of course, the complete focus of your world at that point was to make sure your needs were met. It was all about you. You were the center of your universe. As you grew, you developed certain expectations, such as whether you would be fed when you were hungry, based on experience. These expectations became the stories you told yourself about how the world worked, and were often easier to accept than your discernment.

Relying on your stories instead of your consciousness became a habit, a de facto auto-pilot approach to life. For example, if you were hungry and no food was readily available, you probably soon discovered ways to distract yourself from your hunger. Instead of trusting your intuition, or discernment, you became a master at avoiding it altogether. In this light, drugs and alcohol can be seen as reliable ways to numb out.

These early experiences initiate your feeling of separation from your higher self. When you really look into a newborn's eyes, you will see its soul shining with great clarity. This pure awareness is the nature of the higher self. Its light sparkles unquenchably from the body's first breath to its last. Your higher self is unchanging, unceasing, immortal and drenched in unconditional love. It is your essence, who you really are.

*So my higher self is what makes me magnificent? No matter how many mistakes I make, or how many people I hurt, my higher self never changes, never grows tired of me, or angry, or abandons me in disgust?*

Never. It is with you right now. Actually, you and your higher self are not separate at all. As Buddha said, "You can explore the universe looking for somebody who is more deserving of your love and affection than you are yourself, and you will not find that person anywhere."

*I sure don't feel very magnificent.*

That's because of the fear-based stories you have been telling yourself since you were small, the ones you made up to explain the world.

# 4 "Isness" and the Illusion of Control

If you hold onto the handle, she said, it's easier to maintain the illusion of control. But it's more fun if you just let the wind carry you.
– *Brian Andreas*

*But without stories of how the world works, nothing would make sense!*

Please do not confuse the need for context with a need for particular stories. Context creates a container of meaning out of the incomprehensible infinity of the multiverse. A growing number of physicists are convinced that the universe – namely space, with all the matter and energy it contains – does not even begin to encompass the whole of reality. According to quantum theory – the deepest theory known to physics – our universe is only a tiny facet of a larger multiverse, a highly structured continuum containing many universes.

Understanding how the container called context distills a tiny piece of the "isness" of the multiverse into your experience is a fundamental aspect of growth and healing, and is a core component of this book. We define "isness" as how the world actually is, as opposed to how your stories of fear and lack (what some call scarcity consciousness) tell you it is.

For example, many people are taught that the world is a cold, cruel place filled with implacable forces of evil. In addition, this story insists that most people are out to take advantage of you, so you must be constantly on guard. Trust is for fools. These are all stories that people mistake for the truth. Those lost in fear predictably act in ways that seem to make them safer, even when such actions come at the expense of other people's safety.

None of these stories makes the world an evil place, though it can certainly seem that way. When hurricanes howl, or earthquakes rumble and shake, devastation is the inevitable result. Many beings experience great suffering. Still, such events don't make the world evil.

As you raise your consciousness, you become able to make decisions based more on the "isness" of the situation, rather than on your fear-based stories. Perhaps you'll choose not to live in an area prone to severe earthquakes, or at least you'll choose to live in an earthquake-resistant structure at least a little distance from known fault lines. You might choose not to settle in coastal areas where hurricanes can cause devastation. The world will seem less chaotic to you as your ability to become present to the "isness" grows, for it is only in the now moment that true discernment is possible.

For now, let us examine how your stories came to run your life. Early on, someone, perhaps your Mother or Father, maybe a sibling or a friend, failed to behave according to your expectations. You were no doubt surprised, even shocked, and then you became disappointed, even angry. You expressed your anger with your whole body. This is commonly called having a tantrum. While you've been taught that throwing a tantrum is self-indulgent, the truth is that it also feels really great! For a little while, you get to prove, at least to yourself, that you are the center of the universe, and your issue is the only one that matters!

For example, one of life's guilty pleasures is having bouts of indignant rage. It's an intense adrenaline rush, and for many people the immediate result appears worth the consequences of the tantrum. Maybe that's why you continue having explosions of rage throughout your life, often at a great cost to any opportunities for intimacy.

*I'm offended by that! I pride myself on my self-control. I despise people who fly into a rage at the slightest provocation.*

If you believe that, you are simply fooling yourself. We certainly meant no offense when we pointed out that you engage in these kinds of emotional outbursts. Please, take a few deep breaths and remember that we are on your side.

*OK, I apologize for getting testy. I kind of surprised myself.*

No worries. Let's get back to our discussion. After you had experienced a series of these angry episodes, your illusion of control over the situation vanished. You felt powerless. You began to realize that your expectations about other people and the circumstances of the world around you do not translate into control over those people or circumstances. Your becoming enraged triggered another's rage against you, resulting in further physical and emotional wounding. It is only when you see this cycle that you can finally begin to understand the process that results in such outbursts.

*Wow, that sounds uncomfortably similar to something right out of my own childhood.*

Of course it does. We're your higher self, remember? We were there. In any event, it didn't take too long to figure out that expressing rage was not working to fulfill your desires, and you began casting about for other strategies. At this point you started school, and began acquiring a larger pool of experientially-based knowledge. Surely, you thought, this is the answer! If you could just learn enough about how people and the world worked, you would at least be able to predict behavior, even outcomes. That would be almost as good as control, wouldn't it?

That became the paradigm. Trust only what you've learned through direct experience and education as the foundation for what is real. Whatever you do, never rely on anything other than your five senses. The rest is untrustworthy, as it has not been proven effective in controlling your world. You've already gotten in trouble by relying on your intuition. Using direct experience is a rational, linear approach to the issue of how to determine beliefs that are both safe and effective.

So, can you think of some stories you've created that help you discount or even ignore your intuition in order to live in a rational world?

*That feels like a loaded question. I'm not sure how to answer that.*

We are not trying to set you up, if that's your concern. Still, it remains a vital question. You see, until you take on the question of what you truly believe, you can never get to *how* you came to believe it. It's crucial to thoroughly grasp both the what and how of your belief structures before you can realistically make *conscious* changes. Most belief systems are not open to self-inquiry, and that is where they limit themselves. In any case, the question still stands; does a rational, linear, reductionist approach to life seem to be working for you?

*As far as I'm concerned my life works just fine, at least in certain areas. I have to admit, though, that neither my personal experience nor my education serve me in all situations, especially around my intimate relationships. However, I'm not ready to abandon my rational world and suddenly start relying only on my feelings as a guide to every situation. After all, wouldn't that leave me open to the manipulation of anyone who wanted to control me?*

That certainly is the fear that runs you. This is essentially what you have been doing your whole life, though you denied the validity of any feelings originating beyond your five senses. While relying on intuition and feelings without using discernment definitely leaves you open to manipulation, why would you ever consciously turn over control of your feelings to anyone else?

That's certainly not what we are suggesting, nor are we saying you should rely on your feelings as your only guide. Your feelings and discernment are two very different forms of perception. They are both essential elements of your being, though many people confuse them and think they have to choose one or the other.

Drunk with Wonder

# 5 Emotional Balloons

The soul would have no rainbow had
the eyes no tears.

— *John Vance Cheney*

Feelings are your natural emotional responses to the "isness" of your life, which we define as whatever events and circumstances are experienced before you assign them meaning. Events happen. Circumstances are what they are. This is the "isness." How and what you feel about these events and circumstances determines your reactions to them.

From your earliest moments, your family and society conditioned you to react in specific ways to the "isness" of the moment, including when to be happy, when to be sad, when to be angry, and especially when to be silent. While there are powerful, potent emotions that arise out of the millions of years of evolution, most of the feelings that you experience (or, more likely, repress) are rooted in the stories you believe about yourself and the world.

True feelings often conflict with the rules that society, or your family, imposes on you around what constitutes acceptable expression of your emotions. Remember these? "Children are to be seen, not heard! If you don't shut up, I'll give you something to cry about!" As a result, most people begin having difficulty recognizing their true feelings when they are still quite young, and so never learn anything about healthy, appropriate emotional expression. How can you express your emotions in positive ways if you don't even know what you're feeling?

*I never thought about it that way, but I see your point. I was taught that becoming emotional was a sign of weakness, and that I would be exploited if I authentically expressed my feelings.*

Interesting how that works. Long ago, the dominant culture decided that, in the name of being civilized, it would be better to ignore or even bury most emotions. In essence, it became wrong to feel. Yet your emotions fuel whatever passion lives in you. Notice that no one ever speaks of thinking their passion; it's always about feeling it.

We've seen that human beings are inherently emotional. You're born with the ability to express all of your emotions, allowing painful experiences to pass through with a minimum of trauma before easily returning to your naturally joyful state of being. You are hard-wired to express your feelings in healthy ways, and will do so unless you're "taught" to do otherwise.

It's as though you are born with natural "re-set" buttons that you access by fully allowing your feelings to express through your body. It's not until you begin to have some of your feelings made wrong or unacceptable, particularly their full expression, that you begin "stuffing" them. It's as though there is a big balloon inside of you into which you shove every emotion you don't feel safe letting out.

When you are young, your intellectual abilities haven't yet fully developed, so you feel a singularly strong connection to your body *as* yourself. When your feelings are made wrong and you're forced to stuff them, it feels as though you are wrong at your core, because you can't separate your feelings from your experience of being. And because your feelings live in your body, when you don't feel safe expressing them, it is as though you are not real, that you don't even exist. Without feeling safe in your own skin, there's nowhere you can go except by numbing out or otherwise distracting yourself.

*Wow, this is amazing! Now I understand why I often feel so hesitant to express my deepest feelings. It had never occurred to me that there might be healthy, appropriate ways to express all of my emotions.*

We wish to make a distinction here. Though there is no doubt that you always have a choice as to how you are with the "isness" of each passing moment, there is no realistic chance for meaningful choice until you learn that it is possible. Most people are actually raised to believe that they don't have many choices about important aspects of their lives.

For example, attending college may seem impossible for someone from a disadvantaged background. Coming from traditional societies in the Mid-East or India, marrying for love may seem hopeless. While it is not easy to transcend stories of fear and lack "in the twinkling of an eye," people do it all the time. For everyone else, it takes years of dedicated effort, of reflection and healing, to come to a deep and abiding peace within.

As more people come to live from this place, they serve as beacons of light, inspiring others by illuminating the simple yet profound truth that everyone has a choice *in this moment* about how they are with the "isness." We repeat this for emphasis: it is *only in this moment now* that anyone can be the change they wish to see in the world.

In any event, by the time you reached middle school, you were better at filling your balloon than naturally expressing your feelings. And you know what happens to a balloon when it gets too full, right?

*Well, I suppose it bursts.*

Certainly it can, but if it's a strong balloon it will reach a certain pressure and then start leaking on everyone around you. And who might that be? Think about it. Who do you usually unload on when your balloon gets too full?

*That's easy. It's almost always my family and friends, the people closest to me. I rarely let loose on a stranger.*

And so it is with most people. You hurt the ones you love, because at some level you see them as safer than people you don't know. Unless you express your feelings in the moment, or regularly empty your balloon in safe and appropriate ways, accumulated feelings turn into toxic sludge, blocking your ability to access your natural powers of discernment. Remember that discernment, as opposed to judgment, allows you to distinguish between the "isness" of any given event and the meaning you give it. It's about using your natural knowing to make choices that work in your life. The challenge is to make healthy choices by first learning to appropriately process your feelings, so they support, rather than sabotage, your discernment.

*OK, maybe I could do a better job of expressing my feelings, but I still don't see what that has to do with determining what I make my life mean.*

Your life means only what you choose to make it mean. And you cannot make meaningful choices when you're unconsciously being run by your feelings. You must be able to completely feel all of your emotions in order to become centered and grounded in the root of your Being. Until you are willing to lovingly examine and unconditionally accept the seeming maelstrom of your disowned feelings, you will continue to be run by them.

Let us make a distinction here. The scientific method is great for describing the physical universe. It is an enormously valuable tool for learning about the world, and for developing technologies to extract benefit from that world. If you want to know something about matter, energy, space or time, explore the sciences. Design your own experiments. The scientific method has even been successfully applied to some of the social sciences, though humans are still in pre-school in these areas of investigation.

However, many of the most important aspects of human life are clearly outside the purview of science as you know it. Love, trust, friendship, humor, intuition, creativity, music, beauty, poetry and culture are just a few of these. Have you ever had a feeling of connection with someone you've just met? Have you ever been deeply moved by a poem, a song, a work of art or an act of compassion? Have you ever been in love? Have you ever known, really *known* that a particular course of action was right for you, and then acted on it, and you were correct? Have you ever been in a place or a situation where you suddenly felt a tingle in your spine? You know, when the hair on the back of your neck stood up and you *knew* danger was near? All of these are examples of intuition, or natural knowing. Do you see the difference?

*So you're saying that discernment is more of an art than a science?*

We are saying, quite specifically, that discernment is a bridge to the higher self. For most people, at least in Western society, the longest distance in their lives is the space between their heads and their hearts. This is where people's lives fall apart, or never come together in the first place.

This "disconnect" is the chasm that swallows hopes and dreams, confusing even the best logical processes. It leaves many wondering why they can't manage to break free of their self-sabotaging patterns of behavior and create the results they so desperately long for.

Reawakening your natural discernment, and learning to trust its phenomenal power, is the most effective way we know to bridge the gap between your heart and your head.

# Feelings

It's normal to feel your feelings
It's OK to feel them all
It's fine to feel fear
On this Earth plane
Where lurk many dangers –

Our bodies get scared
And feel constricted,
Muscles tight
Breath hot…

But half the discomfort
Or more, like as not
Comes from our belief
That we shouldn't be afraid,
That it's inappropriate
Or worse,
That we're cowards –

It's OK to feel my feelings
All the way through
To the core of my soul,
Though sometimes
I'm frightened
Of losing control…

Sometimes I'm scared
Of feeling endless pain,
But what I'm most scared of
Is feeling my feelings…

So I own it,
Breathe deeply,
And feel some more…
It's OK –

# 6 The Power of Stories

> If you think you're enlightened, go spend a week with your parents.
>
> – *Ram Dass*

*What you're saying about discernment makes sense, and I see how I can use it way more than I do in my day-to-day life. However, I am curious about what role discernment plays in creating beliefs.*

As it happens, your beliefs and your discernment are deeply intertwined. Remember, we have defined discernment as that point where knowledge and instincts intersect. How and what you believe manifests in every aspect of your daily life. If you've been taught to believe that you're not good enough, you tend to make choices that reinforce that belief. It's your discernment, however, that is ultimately at the core of your beliefs.

*It doesn't seem that way. It's not as though I stop to consider my intuition before every decision I make.*

Actually, you do, although it happens so quickly and automatically you are rarely aware of it. Most people define the word "belief" as referring only to some pre-packaged set of religious topics. In fact, just like every other person on Earth, you possess your very own comprehensive system of beliefs. These range from those that address the big questions of life all the way down to the miniscule and mundane. You just don't think of your beliefs as arbitrary. Instead, you probably think of them as your "story."

*What do you mean by story? This is my life we're talking about, not some story.*

We mean no disparagement. It is essential to understand that everyone has stories. They are the context, or container, that gives meaning to your life. These stories come from many places, including your parents, religious training, education, interactions with others, and most importantly your interpretations of all of these encounters. These stories include not only those which others intended for you to learn, but also those which you learned by observing how others behaved as well as by direct experience.

For example, you were told not to yell at your brothers, then observed your parents quite often yelling at each other as well as at you. In other words, those who you depended on most for your emotional and physical well-being could not always be counted on to match their actions to their words. They were often incongruent, as in, "Do what I say, not what I do."

*As you know, I got that a lot when I was young, though I don't understand how it became the foundation of my belief system.*

You're certainly not alone. Understanding this concept can be elusive in its simplicity. The reality is that your stories become the very fabric of your existence. You depend upon them for continuity in what you experience. Without your stories, large and small, you would have no perspective, no context, no meaning whatsoever. You almost always make choices that are aligned with your core stories. You open up to new possibilities whenever you are able to put these stories into a larger perspective, with full awareness of the causative elements. We can't emphasize strongly enough that it is your absolute belief in your stories that serves as the basis for every single choice you make in your life.

Being raised in an environment where people are not congruent makes you doubt your body, your feelings, your natural knowing and your inborn discernment. When you lack such trust, it becomes almost inevitable that you take on stories that damage your innate knowing of your worth as a Divine spark of God.

*Really? I can't imagine any story in my life being so all-encompassing.*

OK, perhaps you can just be in the question for a moment while we look at how your stories affected your life. There are certain facts that can serve as the starting point. You are a Caucasian male of middle age, the eldest of five boys. You were born in Gooding, Idaho in 1949.

Each of these facts gives rise to a specific set of experiences. As an infant, long before you had any consciousness of doing so, you began to draw conclusions about what the "isness" of your life meant, thereby creating your first stories. For instance, for the first two years of your life, you were an only child. Your mother constantly doted on you, playing, talking to and holding you close. In short, she showed her love for you in every way she could think of. For two years, she never left you. Not surprisingly, you formed a story that you were the center of her universe.

Just after your second birthday, the first of your four brothers was born. Not only did your mother need to take care of an infant, within months he developed a series of serious health issues. Your mother's attention, already focused on your brother, became even more so. To you, it felt as though your mother was gone. You were left in the care of a father who, even if he hadn't been working full time, was sorely unprepared to step into the role of primary caregiver. In your young mind, it seemed as though your mother's apparent abandonment must be your own fault. You concluded that you were not enough, or your mother would not have left you.

Desperately lonely, you felt an overwhelming need to return to the center of your mother's universe, but there was no going back. Your father's frustration and impatience reinforced your growing belief that you were not good enough. We wish to emphasize here that these were your stories, what you made the "isness" of those experiences mean. In fact, she did not abandon you. You never missed a meal or being tucked in at night. You just, quite naturally, missed her constant attention. It's easy enough to say, "Get over it," but to a two-year-old, that has no meaning.

*OK, so I was only two when I created that belief. As I grew up, why would I continue believing that nonsense about myself?*

Though you didn't realize it then, you chose to interpret all of your experiences in accordance with those early beliefs. Caught up as any child would be in your own story, your experience of every event in your young life only strengthened this core belief. From your perspective, you simply could not be enough. This became your core story, or context, your deepest belief about yourself.

Some examples of events that served to confirm your belief that you weren't good enough, and never would be, included your family's move across the country to accommodate your father's new job, the birth of other siblings, and the pencil in the eye incident just after you turned six that left you wearing glasses and then enduring the taunts of schoolyard bullies.

Before long, you had such an investment in this foundational belief about yourself that you began unconsciously proving to yourself that you were right. Your unwavering belief in your core story of not being good enough eventually led to a path of isolation. By age 13 you were smoking cigarettes, and by 16 you began even more self-destructive behaviors that, by age 18, came close to killing you.

*But couldn't I have just chosen to act differently?*

Good question. Yes, you *could* have, though without the context of knowing you could make healthier choices, it's not surprising that you did not. It took many years before you came to understand that you had *always* been inherently free to choose from an infinite number of interpretations of the "isness" of your life. When you finally got that you had a choice, you began to deliberately reinterpret your stories with new meanings, gradually setting aside those based on fear and lack. As you continued to make healthier choices, you were also able to let go of the drugs and alcohol you'd used for decades to self-medicate. It was during this period of transition that you began making room to hear our voice.

# Threads of Shame

Threads of shame
Woven so deeply
Into my soul

They color
My memories
In shades of dread

Follow me home
All the days
Of my life

Relentlessly strangle
My self-respect
With each breath

Each moment
I must be
On Guard

To keep the
Flush of shame
At bay

This is no way
To live,
I know

But the threads
Are woven
So deeply…

# 7 The Voice Within

What the caterpillar calls the end of the world, the master calls a butterfly.

– *Richard Bach*

Every person's journey towards discernment contains similarities. Unfortunately, most people devote more attention to deciding what to watch on TV than they do to questioning their stories. Clinging tightly to these core beliefs, they don't even consider how they came to believe them. They have no awareness that other choices are available. While locked into these stories, discernment is not even an option.

*Are you saying discernment is the tool I can use to question my beliefs?*

Yes it is, and an extremely potent one at that. Discernment is nothing more or less than learning to listen to and trust your natural knowing. Like many people, you spent so many years ignoring the voice of your heart that you had trouble recognizing it when you did hear it. It even took a while to trust that it was indeed *your* voice.

*OK, I get it. I would like to learn how to use discernment, but the whole idea of listening to voices is a huge stretch. I don't even know where to start.*

Quite understandable, though the truth is that just being *willing* is a start. It takes time and repeated, deliberate choosing to re-open the channels between your heart and your head. We are honored that you would permit us to be your guide. As you now know, the clear awareness of the possibilities becomes a lifelong invitation to spiritual growth. The ongoing challenge is to remember, and progressively open, ever so gently, to the exquisite perfection that is your birthright. Spiritual enlightenment is a Divine state of Being that shines at the core of who you really are.

As you practice listening on a daily basis, you will soon be able to create new connections with people. Some will become your allies, just as you will become theirs, symbiotically supporting each other. One of the greatest gifts in this miraculous universe is the opportunity to share the infinite love in your heart with all those who enter your life.

So, are you ready to take the next step with us?

*I think so. The truth is I'm frightened of whatever it is you might ask me to do. Intellectually, I know no harm will come to me, but I'm feeling pretty uncomfortable right now. I'm actually not sure I can do it.*

We appreciate your candor, as well as your courage. It is said that bravery is action in the face of fear. Everything we will ask of you is meant only to support your growth. Should you feel in danger at any point, you need only speak of it, and together we will re-create safety. We assure you that your heart resonates with the message of hope we bring, and it joyfully awaits your choice, in this moment, to transform your fears into pathways of possibility. Feeling uncomfortable from time to time is an inevitable part of the process.

You see, growth is virtually impossible while you hide out in your comfort zone. All growth requires that you step outside of what's comfortable and try something new. While there is often some uneasiness when facing the unknown, we invite you to see this as an adventurous exploration rather than something to fear. Once again, please remember that we are here to support you.

*Thank you. I feel your support. Let's do this!*

Wonderful. We will begin with an exercise that you can use over and over. With time, if you so choose, it will come to feel very familiar and form a core part of your regular practice in mindfulness.[4] It may feel awkward the first few times, but as you become accustomed to the experience, you will find that it becomes a foundation stone of your growing discernment. Please don't become discouraged if you encounter resistance. Just go with the flow, as best as you can, and see where it leads. Trust that you are safe, and that you will know if you need to momentarily return to your comfort zone.

# Drunk with Wonder

# 8 An Exercise in Mindfulness

Breathing teaches you everything you need to know – right under your nose.

– *Gay Hendricks*

Find a quiet place where you can focus on this exercise, without distraction, for at least 15 to 20 minutes. Make sure you are comfortable, but not so much so that you drift off to sleep. Read through the following exercise at least once before you actually do it, so you know what to expect. You may want to write some key words on an index card. You might even pre-record the exercise, and then play it back. If you do this, you will not need to open your eyes to read anything. These aids will serve as reminders, facilitating the process.

Consider choosing one or the other, and let's begin:

Take a moment to close your eyes and focus deep inside. Notice your inner dialog, all the things your mind wants to think about, the endless issues competing for attention. Without giving them any energy, observe how easily, and perhaps even insistently, your issues pop into your consciousness. These thoughts may include responsibilities, worries about people you love, financial issues, maybe a "to do" list. Perhaps terrorists, war, famine or environmental concerns such as global warming, earthquakes or tsunamis are causing concern.

Take your time, allowing yourself to release each issue as it arises. Imagine them floating in a bubble. As they come around to the front of your awareness, acknowledge them, then gently say, "Not now," and put that topic aside for a little while. There is no need to worry;

you can always pick them up again after the exercise. As your practice continues, you may notice that you have fewer, less intrusive issues.

As your mind empties itself of all thoughts, cares, concerns and distractions, dive deeply into the stillness. External noises drift into the background, internal chatter grows quiet, and you may begin to notice bodily sensations. Simply allow them to be. Acknowledge the amazing ability you have for monitoring your being. Also acknowledge any discomfort, and be grateful for the purpose it serves. Without your ability to experience pain, you would be unable to react to the warning it provides.

Are you comfortable? If so, offer thanks. Notice how it feels to experience a healthy balance, to be the owner of such an exquisite vehicle. Notice, too, as judgments come up, how your inner dialogue may say things such as, "Yeah, but it would be more magnificent if I could lose some weight!" Or, "If I were only taller, thinner, prettier, stronger…." Again, gently recognize these judgments and set them aside.

It may be tempting to stay in this quiet, comfortable place, but when you are ready, move your focus even deeper, to that part of you that is your essence. Simply notice your breath, the wonderful sensation of being. Become aware of that part of you that guarantees you breathe while sleeping, that revitalizes every cell of your body without any conscious effort. Can you imagine deliberately guiding all of your body's functions? Give thanks that these housekeeping chores are dealt with below the realm of your conscious mind. Trust that your autonomic nervous system will always take care of your body. Use this trust to sink even deeper, knowing you are in a safe and nurturing place.

As you rest quietly in your essence, observe how it extends past the limits of your body out into the universe, beyond time and space. Notice that you are an integral part of All-That-Is, that you are seamlessly connected with all consciousness, your essence flowing like a wave upon an endless ocean of being. This vast ocean has many names, including the ocean of joy, the great central sun and the infinite field of pure potential.

Let go of any judgment you may hold about your thoughts or their consequences. Know that you are safe here. Whether or not you are aware of it, you are an exquisitely precious manifestation of unconditional love. Just for this moment, please set aside all you've ever been told about an angry, judgmental God, about good and evil or heaven and hell. Allow yourself to sink into this infinite ocean. What does your heart tell you? What do you discern?

Consider the awareness contained within your being, and its ability to create art, music, poetry, great novels, philosophy and the sciences. Given the glorious miracles we are capable of, how much more must the infinitely greater Oneness of All-That-Is encompass? If the sum total of all information contained in the infinite holographic multiverse indeed exists, then how could it not be in the form of infinite Awareness? Set aside any logical arguments just for this moment. What can you discern?

If this Awareness understands more about you than you do about yourself – has experienced every moment of your existence, every thought, every emotion, even knows what it is to be a cell in your body, the ground upon which you walk and even how it feels to be a tear rolling down your cheek – how much compassion might this Awareness have for you? If you were willing to merge with the sublime ecstasy of this ocean of joy, how intimate a relationship could you have?

For just this moment, please set aside all your questions and objections, and just *be*. Allow yourself to relax into our last question, and feel everything that comes up for you. What do you discern? Rejoice in the grandeur of this moment. Bask in the infinite wisdom of the choice you are now making. Know that this is your birthright!

Once you feel as though you are resting comfortably in the ocean of joy, totally immersed in the Oneness, take some time to fully enjoy the ecstasy. [5]

Now, gradually start coming back. Notice your breathing and the sensations in your body. Open your eyes and look around. When you feel ready, get up and stretch, perhaps take a short walk. When you feel grounded in your body, please share a bit of your experience.

*Well, for starters, it feels a bit challenging to return to the world of words. That was a truly amazing experience. I'm still feeling such profound peace, as though I'm cradled in the bosom of the sweetest love. And I had the oddest sensation, as though I was somehow connected to many other lifetimes. Is that what is meant by reincarnation?*

It is indeed, dear one. Welcome to the spiritual path.

## Live the Breath

With every breath you take,
Live the breath –

Every time you blink,
See the darkness and the light –

With every thought you make,
Think of love, of forgiveness, of peace –

Every time you smile,
Know that God lives in your heart –

Thank yourself for every sunset,
Every heartbeat, every moment of time –

Believe that you are Life incarnate
With every breath you take –

# 9 The Dance of Reincarnation

> I know I am deathless. No doubt I have died myself ten thousand times before. I laugh at what you call dissolution, and I know the amplitude of time.
>
> – *Walt Whitman*

*This is really different from anything I've ever experienced. I understand now what you mean by discernment, and I can see how important it will be in examining my beliefs.*

That's great. Now, let us begin that examination by holding up a mirror to your existing beliefs and using your newly remembered powers of discernment to notice what still resonates as true for you.

*That sounds wonderful, but I must admit I'm struggling with the idea of reincarnation. I believe I'll be able to accept all of this more fully if I could just get past that.*

This is a big issue for you, isn't it?

*It is by far the most troubling one I've encountered. So much seems wrapped up in this subject. There's the whole notion of each person having his or her own soul. But is it really their soul, or is it just someone else's soul that's been recycled? And how about karma? If I'm not good enough in this life, will I come back as a sewer rat, or even a cockroach?*

Of course not, at least as long as you "Don't let your karma run over your dogma."[6] Actually, you could choose to come back as an amoeba, a slime mold or even a rock, but we completely understand your confusion. What you're referring to is a melding of several different stories. The difficulty comes from the fact that the pieces you have woven together don't have any continuity. In order for any story to actually work, it has to be logically consistent, at least internally. Let us see if we can untangle this knot that binds you so tightly.

*It's true that I've heard a variety of stories, and every one of them claims to be the one truth. Maybe that's why I'm confused, though I've always tried to judge what feels right.*

Aha! Right there we see two problems.

*What do you mean?*

Judging and feeling.

*Wait a minute! I thought that's what we've been talking about. Isn't that what we just explored in the exercise?*

This is a perfect opportunity for clarification. In the first place, it is important to understand the power words hold to either support or sabotage you.[7] As the great writer Samuel L. Clemens (Mark Twain) said, "The difference between the right word and the almost right word is the difference between lightning and a lightning bug." In our journey together, we will choose our words very carefully, as they are far more powerful than most people realize.

The choice of words profoundly impacts the outcomes manifested through communication. Begin noticing how you use language to describe your moment-to-moment experience. If you find yourself saying things such as, "I'm having a terrible day," stop. Consciously change the word "terrible" to the word "challenging." Look for the gifts in every moment.

What we have been exploring is discernment, not judgments or feelings. Judgment is simply bias passing itself off as discernment. As we've already discussed, feelings are emotional responses to the "isness" of your life, which are conditioned upon the stories you tell yourself. These stories create context, or meaning, out of the "isness."

Feelings are not the same thing as discernment, though they are a glorious part of what makes you human. Further, when you are able to authentically own and feel your emotions, they can serve as a bridge into the clear seeing of discernment. Remember, discernment is about hearing, and then applying, the still, small voice within your heart, the voice directly connected to the One Heart. Under virtually any circumstances that could possibly include thoughtful consideration, we highly recommend asking, "What would love do?" before taking action.

So, let's go back to your mingling of stories. Do you see how powerfully words, in this case in the form of stories, shape your experience?

*I do, in a way I wouldn't have believed possible just a short while ago. I see now how my feelings are shaped by my stories, and I'm feeling kind of shaky, as though everything I thought I knew was simply an illusion.*

Fabulous! Though it may not feel safe, stepping out of your comfort zone is the only way to grow. Now that you are opening to new possibilities, let's take a look at the beliefs you hold about souls.

*That's just it. I'm not even sure I believe in souls. I've always heard that each person has a soul that lives on after they die. I know some religions teach that the soul is eternal, that it has always existed, even before the person was born. It then somehow enters the body and experiences that person's life on this plane, eventually floating away to some non-earthly place when that person's body dies. It retains the essence of the person, without existing in the physical world, and is judged for whatever it did on Earth.*

OK, let's stop right here and go back to your quiet place. Take all the time you need to find that part of you that is connected with All-That-Is. Be aware of any inner dialogue. Gently set aside your thoughts and become completely present in this now moment. Ask yourself, "What can I discern about the existence of my soul?"

*What I'm experiencing is that some part of me does feel connected. It is beyond time and space. It doesn't seem to fit the kind of soul I describe, it's more like a connecting point, a knowing that I am part of All-That-Is, and that it's all part of me. It's as if I already know all the answers, and all I need to do is figure out the questions.*

Does that surprise you?

*In some ways it does. I guess I wasn't quite sure what to expect. In this moment, I'm certainly noticing some excitement about this path we're on.*

Just breathe into the excitement and enjoy the ride. It's called life!

And remember that the universe is holographic, so every part of it, including you, contains the essence of the whole. You are not separate from the universe. Instead, you are actually one aspect of the interconnected totality of All-That-Is. From this place of connection, just listen to your heart. Ask yourself if the old stories of a fearful, jealous, judgmental God who punishes with hellfire and brimstone seem consistent with the all-knowing, omnipresent, infinitely loving source of universal life energy that you are experiencing.

*So you're saying I won't be condemned to an eternity of suffering if I don't submit to a particular deity, or follow a dogmatic form of worship?*

Of course not! Actually, if you read the words of Jesus and Mohammed, the two teachers about whom these stories are most often told, you'll find that neither of them wanted to be worshipped. Having their words venerated beyond the essence of their actual wisdom was never their intention. Fixating on the words alone, rather than on their deeper meaning in the full flowering context of the teaching (as in the admonition to believe every single word of the Bible or burn eternally in Hell), is the dogmatic path.

These wise ones, including others such as Buddha, led humble lives, entreating their followers to listen to the stillness of nature and their own hearts. Their core teachings had nothing to do with placing themselves above all others as Divine beings. Instead, they centered on the Divinity of all humans, particularly the precious spark of God in each human heart. These great teachers invited introspection, just as we are suggesting here, to discover the true nature of Being. This discovery is an inside job, not some externally mandated truth.

*So, do I have a soul?*

Listen to your heart! What do you discern?

*Up to now, my concept of a soul was about something separate and apart from me. What I'm discerning now, however, is wholeness and unity. In fact, separation appears to be nothing more than an illusion. It's not so much that I have a soul, it feels more as though I am a soul. A soul experiencing the miracle of life through a body.*

Yes! You've got it!

# 10 The Illusion of Separation

> Life is one, said the Buddha, and the Middle Way to the end of suffering in all its forms is that which leads to the end of the illusion of separation, which enables man to see, as a fact as clear as sunlight, that all mankind, and all other forms in manifestation, are one unit, the infinitely variable appearance of an indivisible Whole.
>
> – *Christmas Humphreys*

*You've talked about reincarnation. Does that mean that if I've lived through a particular life, then come back as someone else, my soul is still intact?*

You are assuming that a "soul" is the same thing as an individual, that somehow All-That-Is has subdivided into separate beings, each identified as a soul, carrying a separate individuality forward from one life to the next.

In truth, it's more like consciousness itself is one vast fire, with each individual a tiny spark dancing out of the flames for a brief time before falling back into the fire and once again becoming indivisible within it. Eventually, more sparks may jump from the fire, but does it really make sense to think of any of these sparks as a reincarnation of the first? It may carry within it a bit of the essence of the original spark. It may even have within it the potential to be all that the fire is. For any one spark's brief lifespan, however, the momentary manifestation of its infinite potential is contained in its arc across the sky. The spark is as vital to All-That-Is as the fire itself, for what is a fire without sparks?

Where do you suppose the illusion of separation originally came from? Here you are in a seemingly discrete water-filled sack you call a body. You have experienced being alone, without another soul around. You often feel emotions that you don't seem to share with others, affirming your belief that you are separate. The appearance of separation, at least on a physical level, seems pretty straightforward, doesn't it?

*Well, yes, I guess so.*

Now, imagine for a moment that you are God. Of course, that is precisely what we've been saying. We're talking about an undifferentiated God, a God before time and space, a God that simply is. A Oneness that has no experience of being, because there is no subject or object, no context, just pure "isness" or Beingness. This God has infinite power over nothing, because nothing exists to have power over. We know this can be a challenge to imagine, because you embody both subject and object, and so this gives you context. The concept of nothing, no thing but "isness," is completely contrary to your experience of being. Is this clear?

*So, God is nothing but "isness"? If I understand you, I sure wouldn't want to be God. It sounds beyond boring.*

You're missing the point. With no subject or object, no sense whatsoever of a separate self, there is no one at home to experience boredom. The truth is, "Thou Art God," and you experience boredom only if you choose to. As you let that sink in, we ask you to consider whether you really are bored, or perhaps if what you are feeling is fear of owning your magnificence. For now, we ask you to focus on opening your heart and mind to this next part, because this is the key that will unlock your understanding of all that will follow.

In order for God to experience anything, there had to be something to experience, right? A creator must have something to create. And, in order for God to express the unlimited, unconditional love that God is, some parts of that creation had to *appear* to be separate from the rest. Love, as you experience it, is the manifestation of a relationship, and for any relationship to exist, there must be an "other" to relate to, and therein lies part of your purpose in being.

Since, by our definition, God is All-That-Is, then every thing, every particle of matter, every unit of energy, every living creature, every increment of space and time, are all uniquely exquisite parts of God. Please, take a moment to really "grok"[8] the truth of this in the deepest part of your being: "Thou Art God!"

When God created a universe to experience, God necessarily also created duality (separation into self and other), duration (time) and context (meaning). For light to have meaning, there must be darkness that light can illuminate. For there to be up, there must be down. For pleasure to exist there must also be pain. For love there is fear, and for life, you have death. By providing the illusion of separation, duality gives context to All-That-Is.

Remember that duality is itself an illusion, a construct designed by God-As-Us to experience the dynamic tension of up and down, right and wrong and so forth. The tension may last a very long time, and have many permutations, before it reaches resolution. Therefore, the purpose of your existence can be, if you so choose, to move beyond separation and to re-connect into your wholeness.

The whole concept of an eternal, individual soul comes from the belief that separation is real, rather than an illusion. So, to finally answer your question about reincarnation, our perspective is that you are a window into the consciousness of the One. The God within can remember any number of individual lifestreams, all drawn from the endless ocean of life, love, and joy into which those lives have passed, and out of which new ones are constantly emerging.

*So, this is not really about reincarnation as I was defining it, is it?*

Not as you were defining it, no. In the model you seem to be holding, incarnation is often seen as a judgment. In that model, you are sent one more time around the wheel because you just weren't good enough to complete the cycle in your last incarnation. But, if there is no real separation, then being here *is the very purpose* of creation. Rather than being a punishment, each incarnation is like another ride on the roller coaster of life. Each life is nothing less than the miracle of creation made manifest. It is up to you to choose whether you will cover your eyes and be gripped by fear for the whole ride, or throw your arms in the air and shout with glee at the glory of it all.

# The Bubble of Illusion

The bubble of illusion
Bursts and reforms,
Endlessly fascinating
To Consciousness,

The perfection of the moment
Lost and found
Like seashells tumbling
In the surf

Waves dancing
On the ocean
Chasing each other
Like children lost in play

Following the moon
Into the momentary
Darkness of separation
Only to find the sun

Always rising
Just over the horizon,
The One Heart
Welcoming us Home –

# 11 The Great Passion Play

The surest sign of intelligent life in the universe
is that none of it has tried to contact us yet.
– *Calvin (Calvin & Hobbes)*

As we continue our journey together through *Drunk with Wonder*, we wish to paint a rather different picture of creation and purpose than that currently held by many people. It is our hope that this new and perhaps startlingly refreshing story will prove useful to you in finding a more fulfilling purpose for your life.

Our primary emphasis is synthesizing Hindu, Sufi and Buddhist teachings of the East and Shamanic practices of the West with contemporary scientific thought. Sadly, many of the cultures from which these teachings originally emerged are no longer with us.

*It seems such a shame that so many vibrant cultures would simply vanish.*

Yes, it is indeed a shame, though there is nothing "simple" about their vanishing. But that's a topic for another time. Down through the ages of human history, literally thousands of cultures, along with their languages and an enormously rich legacy of stories, rituals and wisdom traditions have been lost. It is as though they never existed. We share our perspective with you in order to create a context within which to articulate our vision. We believe this vision will help create one of the most profound transformations that humans have ever known.

An ancient story from the West has it that, in essence, the Earth is filled with suffering because of humanity's fall from grace into sin. In these traditions, "getting right with God" can only come through an intercessor such as Jesus. Though the name of the intercessory may differ, similar versions of this story can be found in many religions.

A much different story, one of the highest teachings of the East, holds that Enlightenment consists of awakening to the truth of who you really are, getting off the Karmic wheel of life and thereby resolving the need to ever return to this place of suffering.

*I've heard this. Isn't this a Hindu teaching?*

Yes. This teaching goes on to say that none of this Earthly experience is real, calling it Maya, or illusion. In this context, the ego (defined as a virtual construct of thoughts, feelings and beliefs, nothing more or less than a unique collection of stories) is seen as one of the major obstacles to enlightenment, and many teachings involve overcoming it. In fact, some traditions consider the elimination of the ego to be an essential aspect of attaining enlightenment, as though it was some sort of adversary.

In contrast, Western Shamanic tradition holds that the ego simply needs to be mastered. It then serves as an indispensable ally. In this tradition, a number of worlds are perceived, including the physical one we are familiar with, as well as various spiritual realms extending both above and below this one. Notice how closely this echoes the concept of multiple universes and branch points now favored by many physicists.[9]

A Shaman can travel in a spirit body to these other realms, often in the form of a personal totem animal (such as an eagle, bear or wolf), and have experiences and wisdom teachings which they then bring back and share with their community. While the Shaman may have no sense of ego death as in Eastern traditions, the various initiations they go through commonly include out-of-body or even near-death experiences[10] that open the doors of perception to the imaginal realms of Spirit. We define "imaginal realms of Spirit" as domains manifested through the imagination. Far from being relegated to the world of superstition and myth, both out-of-body and near-death experiences are now understood as a natural part of the human experience.

*If I hadn't just felt cradled in infinite love, I'd be laughing hysterically at the whole idea of being out of my body. And do I understand you to be saying that the imagination can actually manifest things physically?*

We are indeed. If you learn only that your imagination, fueled by your stories, creates your experience, you will truly be able to transform your life.

Many people wonder how reality is made manifest. It is our teaching that all physical manifestation is nothing more than the realization of collective consciousness. We define "collective consciousness" as that state of awareness held by a certain percentage of God-As-Us whose aggregate number is capable of manifestation in the world. Whatever that percentage may be in any given situation (and we hold that identifying the number is not relevant to our discussion), it is this cumulative power that has the ability to directly affect the physical world.

*So how do I consciously create intention that not only fulfills my desires, but also holds a vision for the benefit of all creation?*

Conscious creation through the imagination begins with the language used in giving voice to the initial vision. The desired outcome remains just that, a desire, until given the energy required to affect physical reality. Desire, coupled with specificity and fueled with deep passion, are the key ingredients used to create the world. In other words, be very careful what you wish for, as you may get it.

Your highest choice is always your heart's desire, and it is here, in identifying your highest choice, that most people fall short. In your life you have often felt unworthy, as though you're not good enough for the universe to support you in attaining these lofty goals. The truth is that you are fully worthy of everything you wish to do, be, or have, and your conscious choice of language is a key to manifesting your dreams.

Once you prove to yourself that the universe is indeed in alignment with your highest goals, and that you can manifest, even on a small scale, that which you desire, you begin to create a belief system that you can build upon. Only then can you consciously bring your wildest dreams into your life.

You begin by becoming conscious of the immense power of words. We reference the work of Robert Tennyson Stevens,[11] and suggest that time spent on this subject will help you both to identify and realize your deepest desires. To grok the power of the spoken word and its ability to either support or sabotage your desired outcome is an essential component of conscious language. The use of words such as should, could, would, can't, won't, don't, but, if and many others sharply weakens your ability to influence the manifest world. Words such as can, will, love, am, choose, have and create greatly strengthen this ability.

*This seems so simple. I think that's where my mind butts in with cynicism. If it was so simple, why isn't everyone doing it?*

The idea is simple; most great ideas are. And that's the point, everyone, including you, is doing it all the time. As the saying goes, "The universe happily rearranges itself to accommodate your picture of reality." It's another way to say that you create your experience out of the beliefs and stories you hold. It may seem obvious, but we want to strongly emphasize here that all of your beliefs and stories are held within the crucible of language. Therefore, we urge everyone to learn as much as possible about the importance of using conscious language in manifesting your highest goals. "Change your thinking, change your life"[12] may sound like a platitude, but that makes it no less true.

*So you're saying that my use of language is the mechanism by which my thoughts become manifest?*

Exactly, and we wish to emphasize that it is your inner dialogue as much as your outer that creates your experience of reality. We present this brief, incredibly simplified discussion of Eastern and Shamanic concepts in order to give you a context for the vision we have to share. You see, we are all God/Goddess. In the beginning, and in the end, there is only God. There is no one, no thing, no place, no time that is devoid of God. From our perspective, this entire universe is but one breath, one heartbeat of God, and consciousness is at play in this amazing sandbox called Earth.

*But if we're all God, why would we create pain and suffering?*

The answer is very simple, though you may resist it. As God, we have brought the entire universe into existence in order to create a venue within which to enjoy this vast Passion Play. This meta-story includes a multitude of narratives that encompass many thousands of years and billions of cast members. And that's just on this planet! You even have cast parties between incarnations. We will discuss the details of these gatherings later in our dialogue.

You see, God-As-Us loves nothing more than a good story. Every aspect of life, including evolution, relationships, and choices, represents the full experience of being alive in this moment. Let's face it; people have a real knack for creating drama in their lives. As far as experiences go, life is anything but boring! Which reminds us; do you remember your comment about undifferentiated Oneness sounding boring?

*I do, though I feel rather embarrassed to own it after what you have been saying.*

That's understandable, though embarrassment is simply one of the ways you distract yourself from the deeper truth. As in, "Pay no attention to the man behind the curtain!" When you think about it from this perspective, it's clear God-As-Us does a rather incredible job of stagecraft, easily able to create a wonderful stage in the form of the physical universe. Why would you ever play small if you're God? You've even made up some amazing costumes. After all, isn't having a body fun, at least most of the time? By creating the illusion of separation, subdividing your God-Self into seemingly individual souls, each with its own sense of self-interest, you have said, as it were, "Let the play begin!"

*Well, it certainly sounds as though we are masters at playing this game.*

You certainly are. Not only masters, but players, directors, stagehands, audience and the clean-up crew. One of the keys to greater awareness is realizing that the story is continually unfolding out of your multi-dimensional selves through your physical bodies. It's written and performed under the direction of your families, communities and cultures. It is crucial that you fully understand, and accept, that awakening into this eternal now moment is always available. Indeed, when this awakening occurs, it can *only* be in *this* now moment. When at last you awaken, it is to the spectacular truth of who you really are. In this awakening, you can easily, and quite literally, re-write your story moment by moment. You are, after all, God incarnate.

*I'm sorry, but in the interest of full disclosure I must tell you that I'm finding some of this really hard to buy into. While I'm doing my best to keep an open mind, some of this seems pretty far-fetched. I mean, how could I possibly be all of these things?*

Your open mind is all we could ask for. It is a most magnificent gift, and we are deeply grateful for your patience. And the answer to how you could possibly be all those things is quite simple: *Thou Art God.* Your limiting beliefs have kept you from grokking this truth. With your heart and mind opening, you are creating Sacred Space with which to awaken to the God within yourself.

Now, let's continue. For millennia the dominant Eastern story has been that the Earth is a place of profound and continuous suffering, and that the wise among you are able to figure out how to get off the wheel of incarnation and stay off. Herewith we propose an alternate story, one that we hope will help shift the focus of your global conversation from fear into love. If this story supports your awakening, then our purpose is fulfilled.

What we wish to share is that all of manifest creation is Sacred and Holy. All that you experience is truly worthy of the infinite love you are, and what you perceive as reality is, in fact, real, not an illusion. Your lives here on Earth are consciously manifested, not at all a fall from grace. As God, you have never made mistakes. You have chosen to experience every aspect of life through your human identities. There are no mistakes! You are not a mistake, and your life is not a punishment!

We do appreciate that life can *feel* like a mistake when experienced in the context of fear and lack that many of you have been raised with. But even the most intense of these stories will eventually be seen as an integral part of the larger picture. Those who choose the path of fear and lack are simply not aware that they have any other choices, but choice is *always* available if you have the eyes to see through the veils obscuring the truth.

# 12 Science and Oneness

At the atomic level the boundaries among biology, chemistry, physics and electronics lose much of their meaning. The sciences start to merge.[13]

Early in humanity's history, a story was made up to explain why fear and suffering appeared to rule you. In effect, the story says that this world, and all its pain, is nothing more than an illusion; a seemingly endless cycle of birth, death and rebirth. And the only way to escape this karmic wheel, as it has been called for millennia, is to live such a virtuous life that no further incarnations are necessary.

We have come to tell you that this awesome miracle of creation in which you live is no illusion. While all religions have negative as well as positive aspects, the whole idea that you are born into the bondage of sinners condemned to live in fear, suffering and eternal damnation – *unless* you are born again through accepting some savior – is nothing more than an elaborate story designed to keep the chosen few separate from, and better than, everyone else.

Those who do not feel as though they are inherently good enough to share in the inifinite bounty of unconditional love are forever seeking approval and status from something or someone, such as a church or a priest, that lies outside of themselves. This belief forms the core of the story that they are separate and alone.

*If I really do get to choose, then of course I choose not to suffer. Who on Earth would deliberately choose suffering? Wouldn't people be furious if they ever realized that we had a choice? I know I would be. It just doesn't seem as though it could be that simple.*

Who are you going to be furious with? Remember, you are continually creating this world. God-As-You has no one to be furious with but, well, you. It's the ultimate cosmic joke that you play on yourselves. You're much like children playing hide-and-seek. You're God, remember, which means that, as with every other aspect of manifest creation, you are *really* good at hiding. If you've ever felt lost and alone, you know that nothing feels quite as fantastic as being found. It's a delicious, incredibly intense adrenaline rush.

The truth is that this world is nothing less than pure love made manifest. That's all it ever is, has been, or will be. The greatest gift you can ever bestow upon yourself is awakening to this truth, to the love you are as life incarnate. *Life is the ultimate gift of love.* As humanity collectively awakens to the immense truth of who you all really are, together we will write a new story, of which *Drunk with Wonder* is only an opening chapter.

Rather than holding the belief that getting off the karmic wheel of incarnation, and thereby off the planet, is the highest attainment, we offer a vision of an Earth where everyone, and everything, is held as Sacred. In this vision, each and every soul is revered for who they really are, with mutual respect and honor for all beings and, indeed, for all creation. Where, instead of longing to escape from here, you enthusiastically choose one miraculous incarnation after another, each life filled with unconditional love of self, family, community, the world and the entire universe.

After all, for those who have awakened, it is *already* heaven on Earth, and always has been. We humbly propose that you all do what you can moment by moment to choose love over fear. You see, you are the ones who created this play, and you can choose to write any story you wish. Let us write a story together, one where love becomes your life experience. It's *your* game. Choose love.

Down through the ages, wisdom teachings have repeatedly emphasized that you are all brothers and sisters, and deserve to be treated with unconditional love and respect. Although the often-stated Golden Rule, "Do unto others as you would have them do unto you," has much to recommend it, we prefer the Platinum Rule, which says, "Find out what others truly desire and give it to them." Your children, and your children's children's children, will thank you.

*What exactly does "writing our own story" mean?*

As we described earlier, what is real for you is your authentic experience of each moment. You are single threads weaving through each other into an immense tapestry of infinite possibilities. Every person's experience is real to them, and because you're all interconnected, you can expand these experiences, changing and growing as you are exposed to new perspectives. Since you're resilient (being God, how could you not be?), you are able to stretch past your resistance without breaking. In doing so, you will come to have two perspectives, one from your past and a new one you boldly embrace in *this* present moment.

Once you truly understand this, you have a choice. Every time life pulls you back into your old patterns, you can ask yourself which story you'd rather tell yourself in this moment. Will you stubbornly resist seeing any new reality that presents itself, clinging to the old perspective until you fray or perhaps break? Or will you choose to embrace every opportunity for growth? Adding strand upon strand of fresh experiences, you cast off what no longer serves you and joyfully incorporate this more expansive understanding into your life.

*Are you saying that our experience of reality is based wholly on our stories, and there's no such thing as objective reality? Isn't that the same as the*

*Eastern notion that what we perceive as objective reality is just Maya, an elaborate dream state or illusion?*

Not exactly. As we've discussed, while objective reality is no illusion, your experience of it is indeed based entirely on your stories. With every thought, the field of pure potential is continually collapsing into the now moment. That is why the stories you tell yourself are so vital in creating your moment-to-moment experience.

Science has clearly demonstrated that objective reality, commonly defined as experiential observations that can be independently verified as having the same results, and your experience of that reality, are inextricably linked.[14] Is this the proof that finally will allow you to dismiss the notion that you are utterly alone? Or must you be resigned to the reductionist idea of objective reality that relegates you to live in a world dominated by the old belief that you are separate, and that your actions do not affect anything, let alone *every* thing, on Earth?[15]

What these experiments ultimately demonstrate is the fact that, at the quantum level at least, you are not just passive observers of reality, you truly are shapers of that reality. The very act of observing influences what you experience, so in truth there really is no separation at all!

Since we have just seen that the manifestation of reality and the observation of it are inextricably intertwined, the question then becomes, who is the observer of objective reality? Everyone is, of course, through the medium of your collective experience. Every thing, from humans to rocks, amoeba and stars, experiences some level of what we call objective reality. You are, quite literally co-creators of that reality.

Scientists are still questioning the mechanism allowing individual particles, regardless of distance, to communicate instantaneously.[16] Let us suggest to you that maybe they are asking the wrong question. Perhaps they should be asking if the particles are actually connected in some way that transcends mere physical distance. Can it be that what appears to be two separate particles are, in fact, one? Not just one particle, but rather a singular, holographic manifestation of All-That-Is? If this is so, then all things that appear to be separate entities, including people, are actually multiple manifestations of one essence, one truly inseparable being and so share, at some foundational level, every experience.

*I'm not sure I understand what you mean by collective experience. Are you saying that I share everything I do with everyone else, and vice versa? I don't see how, in sharing an evening with a friend, we necessarily have a collective experience with strangers living on the other side of the world.*

Ah, but you do, though perhaps not in the way you're suggesting. You see, since you are all intrinsically connected, you drink from the same well of experience. Herein lies the rub: when we talk about each of you observing objective reality, not one of you is truly objective. Each of you sees things through your particular set of filters, or stories, which are based entirely upon your experiences. The more expanded your consciousness, the greater your capacity to process your stories and give them meaning. A more expanded awareness also affords you greater opportunities to choose those stories that empower you in creating the reality you desire in *this* now moment.

As to the Western interpretation of the Eastern idea that reality is only a transient dream state, first let us point out that this is an incredible over-simplification of the wisdom underlying these ancient teachings. It is fair to say, however, that the emphasis in the Eastern traditions is on the dream as a dream, and frequently as a nightmare. From this perspective, the goal is to awaken from the dream into a different, less illusory state. The drawback to this perspective is that it devalues the present moment, which by this point you must surely realize is all that ever exists.

# 13 Time and the Eternal Now Moment

> Now he has departed from this strange world a little ahead of me. That means nothing. People like us, who believe in physics, know that the distinction between past, present and future is only a stubbornly persistent illusion.
>
> –*Albert Einstein*

*You keep talking about the now moment as if it possesses special properties, but isn't every moment pretty much the same?*

Only if you're not paying attention. Remember, you have created this endless multi-dimensional playground within which you can choose to experience life as though you are separate and alone. Why would you do that? Simply because it makes the game more fun. By fun, we mean more compelling, more of a thrill ride, like the ultimate roller coaster. You're God pretending you're not, pretending you're lost, even desolate.

You set it up so you'd have a whole universe to explore, complete with what appear to be dragons, good guys and bad guys and all the rest. You have all chosen to play this game, which is ultimately about waking up and remembering that you're God in form. Those of you who choose this awakening have a considerably different perspective than those who choose to stay lost in the drama.

You are passing the "no time" of the eternal now moment by entertaining yourself with this infinite story of endless possibilities. How do you like it so far? The truth is that, right now, you are Spirit in form making it up. You are love incarnate. You love experiencing YourSelf in the infinite ways of Being; you love playing the meta-game of hide and seek; you love forgetting and then awakening, riding this great roller coaster of life while bathing in the perfection of each precious, priceless moment.

This awareness is truly liberation from the illusory but very convincing story that you are discrete packets of energy/consciousness trapped in time and space. You are actually the boundless field of pure potential in which time and space occur, as well as time and space itself. You are *not* separate. This is the great cosmic joke! Every moment of your life, including your awakening, only happens in the now, completely out of time.

*Excuse me? What happens out of time?*

Everything, including forgetting and awakening.

*But, as long as life happens, who cares whether it's in or out of time?*

That's a good point, and you're right. It doesn't matter. However, some people might appreciate knowing that Awakening doesn't really take any time at all. Awakening doesn't happen "in time," it happens now. Once it is grokked that being fully, completely present in the moment is the key to Awakening, tools can be acquired, techniques learned, attitudes adjusted and stories re-written that foster staying present. With patience, intention and practice (that's why it's called a spiritual practice), one inevitably grows towards greater awareness.

*I'm confused again. How can you talk about awakening not taking any time and yet that it has to happen in the present moment? Isn't the present moment part of time?*

Funny you should ask. You see, within the "isness" there is only the eternal now moment. Period. Contained within the eternal now moment is the entire universe as you know it, plus an infinite number of universes of which you have absolutely no awareness, and probably never will. None of you in human form can contain the fullness of the infinite. It would be like trying to contain the world's oceans in a thimble, only more so.

As one tiny example, imagine a world just like this one. Everything is exactly the same, and we emphasize *exactly*, with one exception. The tree in your front yard has one more leaf on it. Or one less. You can extrapolate the endless possibilities from there. Suffice to say that in an infinite multiverse, not only are all things possible, all things are mandatory, or it wouldn't be infinite.[17]

*OK, I give up. I don't begin to understand how there can be no time, let alone this multiverse idea. Can we get back to our discussion about time? For instance, if there's no time, what in the world is my watch doing?*

Sorry to confuse you. Simply put, your watch measures duration. Within this universe, time exists as an inextricable part of space. From an astronomical perspective, describing where a stellar object can be viewed necessarily includes when it can be viewed there. A simple example of this phenomenon would be how the Big Dipper appears to change location in the sky from winter to summer in the Northern Hemisphere. Of course, it can't be seen at all in the Southern Hemisphere, just as the Southern Cross can't be seen in the Northern Hemisphere.

Now, just for the sake of our dialogue, imagine a limitless grid. Not just height and width and depth, but also a fourth axis extending through time. With such a grid, we can plot where this planet has been in space at any point since it condensed out of stardust, or any "when" if you will. The fourth axis of the grid is the "when" we speak of. You call it time.

When you plot a single 3-D moment, such as this one, time is non-existent, for there is no other perspective. It is only when you add the fourth axis, or dimension, by plotting where you've been as well as where you're going, that you step into a larger perspective of the now. From the limited awareness of your 3-D selves, there can truly only be the now. The past is dead, the future merely imagined. Only the now moment is available to you.

*Yikes! That sounds awfully weird to me.*

How so? We're simply giving you a cosmological perspective that is quite familiar to astronomers and other scientists. Nothing weird about it.

*Maybe not to you, but it hurts my brain to try and imagine something so monumentally huge.*

We can appreciate how unsettling it can be to have your world view irrevocably altered by contemplating an immensely larger perspective. However, if you will stay with us on this, you will soon realize that, by using this 4-D grid, you can plot where and when you are at any point in time within the context of the matrix. Right?

*Hmmm, I guess so. But so what?*

Well, you were asking about time, so we are painting this picture in order for you to understand what we are talking about. You live within the context of the matrix of the universe, the where and when that constitutes this moment for you.

*But what about the past and future? Where are they?*

It's all contained within the four-dimensional matrix. Every thing and every when, every possible experience, event and feeling are contained within this matrix. But they're not real for you, not like your present moment. From the perspective of a soul in form traveling through a tiny piece of the matrix that their body inhabits in its lifetime, the past is dead, inaccessible, as though it never had been.

The exceptions, of course, would be any memories or stories you might retain, and any mementos you may have brought with you. The future also remains just out of reach as an infinite cloud of probabilities and possibilities, and remains so until choices made in the present moment create nexus points around which possibilities coalesce into the next present moment, and so on.

*Does that mean that time does not exist between incarnations, at least as we know it? And if that's true, then the soul essence is able to choose each incarnation out of the matrix of infinite possibility?*

Exactly. And that includes every single aspect of your incarnation, including your parents, any siblings and all of your life experiences. Free will occurs within the choices you can make concerning those experiences, including whether you believe you're locked into one destiny.

Between lives, when you're hanging out in the ocean of joy, this entire four-dimensional matrix is equally available. You are not locked into a linear sequence of lives. You can choose to experience a life any *where* as well as any *when* you wish. For example, you can have a life in 1800AD France, then 2200BC Persia, then 2453AD China, and so forth. From our perspective in the ocean of joy, it's all life, and it's all good.

Please be aware that even in this life the future of any present moment is far from preordained. Even stone isn't etched in stone, it simply has a tendency to remain in its present form until enough energy shows up to effect some sort of phase change. This is also called inertia, but that's another story.

The point here is that, to spend time thinking about the dead past or the imagined future keeps you from showing up fully in this moment. And here and now is where all the action is, so if you're distracted, you miss life. Most of you, most of the time, especially until quite recently, have been doing just that, missing out on the awesome joy, freedom and bliss that's available only in the present moment.[18]

## Stealing Moments

Stealing moments
Like pickpockets

We become present
To the siren call of life

Fully awake in
These stolen moments

Glancing furtively around
To see if anyone's noticed -

Not grand theft, perhaps,
But stolen for sure

We rip these
Precious times

From the roots
Of our stories

And flee,
Laughing, into...

Another present moment,
Taken like hunters

Out of the stream of life,
Feasting on the Now...

# 14 Consciousness and Choice

> There are two primary choices in life; to accept conditions as they exist, or accept the responsibility for changing them.
>
> – *Denis Waitley*

*OK, I think this whole time thing is beginning to make sense, though I feel as though my head is spinning. For now, may we go back to the subject of consciousness? You said earlier that higher consciousness would allow me to choose my reality. Can you please explain this?*

When we speak of higher consciousness in this way, we don't mean in a hierarchical sense so much as a more expansive one. For example, someone starting at sea level, and then traveling to the space station, would not automatically know how to be a better person. They would simply have a much greater perspective of their little corner of the solar system. They would be able to see the Earth's curvature, and uncounted stars that are normally hidden by the scattered light of the Earth's atmosphere.

While such an experience would not, in and of itself, necessarily heighten a person's consciousness, it has happened. Edgar Mitchell, one of the Apollo astronauts, returned from his sojourn in space a changed man, so much so that he soon founded The Institute of Noetic Sciences,[19] which today has tens of thousands of members devoted to the scientific exploration of consciousness.

Similarly, higher consciousness is also a shift of perspective. As we have seen, most people still feel as though they are victims of their circumstances and other people's choices. From a higher level of consciousness, it is possible to see that you create your own experience through the choices you make. The most powerful of these involve which stories you listen to, tell yourself and believe in.

Underlying this level of consciousness is the fundamental realization that you are not *any* of those stories. Rather, you are the *author*. This awareness is crucial, as these stories form the context through which you create meaning. You may not be in control of all of your experiences, but you are, by virtue of choosing your stories, in control of how you *interpret* those events. It is your stories that, moment by moment, affect your life experience.

Stories create context. They rationalize the "isness" of your experience, and either support your evolution by furthering your chances of surviving and having progeny, or they don't. Furthermore, your stories either enhance the quality of your life, creating passion and happiness, or sabotage you, creating misery and angst. *It's your choice!*

*What does that mean in practical terms? How does all this affect me?*

It means that even though God-As-Us set life up to appear oh-so-serious, you're actually just like a bunch of neighborhood kids, gleefully playing hide and seek on a warm summer evening. You pretend to be lost and alone simply because it feels so outrageously wonderful to awaken to the underlying truth of who you really are, recognizing that there never was any real separation to begin with.

So, you're at play in an extreme miracle you call the universe, holding onto your role as though your very life depended upon it. Each day, more of you are awakening to this open secret and winking at each other, as if to say, "OK, I get it, this is truly all play, an amazing adventure called life that we get to share as we support each other in our journey." With this realization you get to unconditionally love all of creation, including those who choose to stay lost in the drama. You understand that they are not victims, even though they may go to great lengths trying to convince themselves, as well as everyone else, otherwise.

One could say that you are playing the most outrageous practical joke on yourselves. Actually, you are a great cosmic punch line as well as the comedian, the audience and the stage. Fear, separation, lack and other perceived negative emotions are self-created, precisely because it's so enormously rewarding, so utterly exhilarating, to come Home again.

*That's it? We create getting lost in fear because it feels good to re-discover love? It just seems as though there should be more to life than that.*

You are disappointed that there is not more to life than living fully? That there is not more to life than, well, living? When you are outer-directed, it seems as though there should always be more somewhere. When you live out of a story that says you are not enough, it seems that "enough" can only be found "out there," whether it be a job, a spouse, a car, a home… it's out there. It must be, because if it isn't, there's no hope at all. Of course, this story only seems to hold true as long as you buy into it.

Try this analogy: Imagine God-As-Us dancing into the illusion of separation as deeply as it's possible to go, through the entire tumultuous journey of reconnection back to the One, and grokking it as the ultimate roller coaster ride. And what's the first thing many of you want to do when you get off a ride like that? Why, you insist on going again.

And that's the trap. As long as you look outside yourself, you continue missing the truth that there is literally no end to the love, abundance and joy available to be experienced. Playing "hide and seek" creates the emotional highs and lows which form a necessary part of duality. This is what gives you perspective on this amazing journey you call life.

We are here to remind you of what you already know, what you've always known deep in your bones, that you are a conscious co-creator of your moment-to-moment experience. After all, as this profound awareness settles into your being and becomes your preferred way of life, you will come to realize it's the only game in town. Whenever you can remember to relax into clear seeing,[20] you'll know that playing this game has an infinite number of delicious, juicy permutations.

Now, here's the exciting part. Stories do not exist outside of some context! So, by choosing love, you will find that love becomes the context of your life. Your experiences will be joyously bountiful, and you will have no desire to become lost again in Fear-Based-Consciousness. As you become anchored in your essence, you will be able to ride the roller coaster of life with an ease and grace you would never have believed possible.

We repeat: the answer to why you are here is simply to experience the wonder of life. Sunrise, sunset, babies, puppies, kittens, art, music, the love for a child only a parent knows, the devotion of lover and beloved – what an astounding miracle it all is! It is profoundly liberating to understand how your stories affect your experiences; especially as you grok ever more deeply how inextricably linked your experience of suffering is to your fear-based stories.

The truth is, all stories ultimately keep you from relaxing into clear seeing. You came here to play! When you get tired of playing, you can rest. When you tire of resting, you can play! Of course you can play without getting tired, and you can rest in the ocean of joy, forever. It is simply about letting go of the illusion of separation, and having fun with this party called life.

One of our favorite ways to play is by doing seva, or service. Everyone who volunteers knows the intense joy that comes from helping make the world a better place. As the amrita of unconditional love begins to spill forth from your opening heart, it must be put to good use. The more love you share, the more love you have to share. It is a never-ending, virtuous cycle.

Remember, dear one, that since you are the author of your script, it is your choice whether to include hardship, suffering and the role of victim, or happiness, satisfaction with life, loving relationships, sufficiency, seva and joy. It's absolutely your choice!

# 15 The Game We Were Born to Play

Life is either a daring adventure or nothing.
– *Helen Keller*

*What you describe sounds so beautiful, especially the part about the devoted lover and the sunsets. You make it seem so enticing, but you forgot to mention divorce, child abuse, cancer and other painful realities. How do you fit starvation, disease and torture into your model of God at play? What can you possibly say to a mother who has just lost her child, or to a victim of war or terrorism? How would you explain this game to a young person facing amputation caused by a drunk driver, or a woman who has just discovered a lump in her breast?*

Oh, dear one, there is so much hurt and fear in your questions! Child abuse, starvation and torture are examples of how, when you remain unconscious victims of your experience, you pass on your wounds. Cancer and other diseases seem to be an almost inevitable result of living in a toxic world, as well as from having bodies that inevitably decay as they age. No matter what the experience, you still have a choice regarding what you make it mean.

In the case of a woman who discovers a lump in her breast, she is at a crucial choice point. The cancerous lump is the "isness." How she is with it is the key. Does she slump into victim consciousness and become a passive consumer of whatever passes for healthcare in her world? Or does she become a proactive co-creator of her care, researching healing modalities that may prove far more successful than standard therapies? Perhaps most importantly, does she choose to see the lump as a potent gift calling her to become fully present with each remaining moment (whether it's four years or 40) of her life?

We have heard people touched by cancer say that it was the best thing that ever happened to them, because it called them to awaken into the moment. They made a choice to love fully, to smell every rose, to adore every sunset, and to hug every friend. Everyone faces challenges in life, dear one. It's how you are with these times, rather than the times themselves, that define you as victim or creator.

Do you suppose God wants these things for you? Do you believe God is capable of loving you unconditionally and yet simultaneously enjoys your suffering? Can you understand that your pain is God's pain, that your tears are, quite literally, God's tears? Remember, Beloved One, there can be no light without dark. Duality gives us context, which gives us meaning. The devotion of a loved one is infinitely more precious when we know that they might not always be around. There are countless stories of individuals who, though suffering enormous pain and loss, have still found the courage to become heroes. Through love, understanding and compassion, these people have still managed to make a difference in the world.

*Whether it's God or God-As-Us, how could any unconditionally loving being allow all these terrible things to happen?*

Ah, your question tells us you still think that God is somewhere up there in heaven, lording it over you mere mortals as He judgmentally makes choices as to who is favored and who is not. That God and humans are separate, and that God is choosing your suffering. For one to truly have free will, or to experience this world at all, there must be options. Do you really think it would be better if God had populated a perfect world with flawless little puppets, everyone with immaculate smiles painted forever on their faces, and no possible imperfection ever disrupting their existence? Would you really want to live in that kind of a "Stepford" world?

If you consider your questions carefully, we think you will discover that you've been trapped in victim consciousness. You see yourself as a helpless child, with God acting as both a loving Mommy and a harsh Daddy who rewards or punishes your behavior. You think it's up to God to meet your needs, that you're incapable of happiness without His largesse. If you fall and scrape your knee, you want God to make the hurt go away, and when that doesn't happen, you get angry with this seemingly uncaring Deity. You think, "If God is omnipotent, and truly loves me, why doesn't He solve my problems?"

*Then why does God allow problems that need fixing in the first place?*

That question, and the pain and anger that drives it, completely ignores the true purpose of creation. You see, God's power was never in question. It was made manifest at the very instant of the universe's birth. In focusing on God's power, you see only one color of the rainbow, hear only one note of a symphony. Yes, God is all-powerful, and God's love is so great and so all encompassing that God-As-Us has chosen to express that power *through* you. It is crucial to understand that all conscious beings have been entrusted with keys to the Kingdom, with the master code of life. By virtue of your birth, you have been given the most precious gift God can bestow, life itself. Yet another miracle, inextricably wrapped up in human life, is the gift of conscious choice.

God-As-Us has created a universe filled with seemingly random events. Many of these events may appear to be profoundly negative, but from your perspective as a conscious co-creator you can, in the blink of an eye, shift to understanding and joyful acceptance. The infinite field of pure potential, an infinite plethora of possible states, includes the free will of every living creature. As we have seen with the Many Worlds

Theory, in many of these states some version of you exists, while in others you do not. In some, you are healthy and happy. In others, your body may be broken, racked with pain, and your sense of self may be lost in victim consciousness.

The deeper truth is that, in an infinite multiverse, all of these different states of matter and energy are not only possible, they're mandatory. If even one event was taken out of the endless panoply of All-That-Is, it would no longer be infinite. The fantastic power of God-As-Us lies in grokking that in every moment of your life you *always* have a choice as to how you define your current condition, and therefore what you make it mean.

All of the individual sparks of God are interacting in real time, and together you create this marvelous, moving tapestry of your lives. No one individual can possibly control the whole, so there will be times when things are going your way, and other times when you feel that, despite your best efforts, all the weight of the world has fallen upon your shoulders.

*How true that is! Sometimes I feel as though my back will break.*

We feel compassion for your back. Please understand that you cannot control the specific choices of even one other individual, let alone the random interplay of the world's seeming chaos. What you can control is your response to the "isness" of your life in *this* now moment. By so doing, you shape the next set of variables around you, influencing the available states of the universe in the ensuing moments, thereby increasing the likelihood that serenity, rather than suffering, will be the outcome. Even if other influences result in painful circumstances, you will still have the ability to make new choices about what meanings you assign to them.

For a fuller understanding of this crucial idea, consider the experience of being a parent. See yourself watching your children, whom you love more than you could ever have conceived possible. As they make choices, sometimes experiencing painful consequences, are you tempted to jump in and protect them from making "mistakes"? Do you long to ease, or even shelter them, from pain? As parents, it is sometimes appropriate to do so.

If you knew, however, that by shielding your children from the consequences of their choices they might be disempowered, and that it might lead to greater pain in the future, would it still be an act of love? Could it possibly be a greater act of love to allow them to learn from this experience, thereby growing stronger? Even though it hurts to see them suffer, can you understand the necessity of allowing them to learn their own life lessons?

If a parent can have such love, then how much greater would the love shown by the Creator be in endowing you with choice? Through you, God experiences all of your states of being, including your feelings, your choices and all of their consequences. Through all living beings throughout this vast universe, even through those things you consider inanimate, God-As-Us experiences the multitude of possibilities that are made manifest by choice.

Parents may feel that their children go out of their way to make things difficult, and many children seem convinced that their parents are intent upon ruining their lives. Since your relationships most often exist within the illusion of separation, they may fail to convey accurately the nature of who you really are. Instead, your relationships reinforce your story that you are separate and alone, that no one understands you. The truth is that everything that you go through, and much, much more, is actually God-As-Us experiencing life at profound levels of compassionate awareness, blissfully being the fullness of unconditional love, forever calling you to a more Awakened sense of Self.

*Are you saying that **all** experience is equally acceptable in God's eyes, that God embraces pain as well as pleasure?*

Not quite. We are saying that God-As-Us *is* pain and pleasure, as well as up and down, light and dark and all the rest of what makes life meaningful. *Every* experience carries within it the potential for learning and growth. *Every* now moment represents a new starting point. So, no matter what experiences you've had in the past, no matter how much you've suffered, you can choose, in this moment, to set aside all suffering and assign new meaning to the circumstances of your life. You *can* rewrite your stories. Though it may not seem that way sometimes, it is truly your highest purpose to do so. This is the game you were born to play, evolving out of fear into love, and then re-writing your stories to reflect this higher Awareness.

One of the most profound truths is that your greatest anguish contains the seeds of your greatest gifts. We are speaking of the miracle of life, which would have no context without sickness and death. Let us begin a journey together to re-write the planetary stories, letting go of fear and suffering and lack as you embrace peace, abundance and celebration. This is not about letting go of duality, even though it may ultimately be illusory; it's about making duality your friend, about seeing it as a gift, as one of the miracles that allows you to experience life in all its paradoxical glory.

## Sidelines

For too long I have sat on the sidelines of my life,
As though waiting for a coach to come along
And order me into the game –

How my ass has gotten sore, my muscles soft,
My dreams of youth no more than bitter,
Pale remnants flapping like a shredded flag
Over the mossy ramparts of my excuses,
Apologies, rationalizations and lifelong fears –

Now I see that it matters not what has gone before,
How many dark eons of night I have sat
Huddled there on the sidelines –

I shall seize the day, as the old ones say
Who have waited too long to be set loose
On the playing field called life –

For I am the coach, the captain too,
And when this day has passed
I will be able to say that I played it well,
Played it full out, played it to the very end –

And when I'm through, they will say of me,
(When they catch their breath)
That my life set an example for them,
And they will rush out onto the field
To play their hearts out,
Just as I am off to do –

I turn back once, to gaze at the bench
Where I spent my youth,
Then onto the field I run,
Ready at last for my
Day in the sun –

# 16 The Dance of Duality

Every explicit duality is an implicit unity.
–*Alan Watts*

Remember, duality is not merely the source of those aspects of life you prefer to avoid; it is also the fount of all things bright and beautiful. Your entire journey of life, from womb to tomb, is made possible by this duality. As just one example, how can you know heights of happiness if you have not experienced the depths of sadness? Even as a baby, one of your first sensations is the discomfort of an empty stomach. It is this primal hunger that not only drives you to seek your mother's breast; it helps create the deep bond of maternal connection. The experience of being nurtured by your mother's precious life nectar as you gaze raptly into each other's eyes is one of the most sublime joys of life.

And so the question remains: if God is the author of duality, then does God really care about your experiences? The answer is an unqualified yes! God-As-Us cares far more than can ever be known in one lifetime. In fact, it is only through pain that you are capable of learning about compassion, undoubtedly one of God's most precious gifts. How do you learn this? Through experiencing compassion for others, it is possible to realize that you *are* God. You see, when you think of God as separate from yourself, you really miss the point. Each of you, in the moment you feel compassion for another by recognizing their pain and opening your heart to them, *becomes* the love of God.

*Sometimes I feel as though there's not enough of that to go around.*

That's an interesting observation.

*How so?*

If you think carefully about what we just said, you will see that we were describing the way in which God's love is abundantly made manifest.

*You mean, by having unlimited compassion for others?*

Just so. You see, God-As-Us created the embryonic universe, described by both sages and cosmologists as a field of pure potential. This field gave birth to all the galaxies, stars and planets, as well as the laws of physics that govern them. It's these laws that led inevitably to life, as well as to evolution, including the evolution of consciousness. Evolution in all its forms continues to unfold. This all began billions of years ago, long before your solar system was born. You see, a huge piece of what you are here to share is that the underlying purpose for everything you experience is the manifestation of God's pure love as life itself. And everyone, including you, are exquisitely precious affirmations of this miracle of love.

If you choose to live your life in fear, jealousy and hatred, that is what you will manifest. If you choose love, reach out in compassion and find the courage to trust, then you will express these qualities. Each moment you choose love, you make more love available to the entire world. As you become more able to express the love you are with each choice you make, you prove to yourself that there is more than enough of everything to go around, that you do indeed live in an infinitely abundant universe.

DRUNK WITH WONDER

# 17 The Power of Choice

> How you choose to respond each moment to the movie of life determines how you see the next frame, and the next, and eventually how you feel when the movie ends.
>
> – *Doc Childre*

*It sounds as though it's all up to me, that unless I choose love it won't happen. Am I the only one responsible for determining whether the whole planet is one big picnic, or literally Hell on Earth?*

Of course, full planetary manifestation is the sum total of everyone's choices, not just yours. While each person contributes to the whole, history has clearly shown that some contributions are more influential than others. For example, Genghis Khan, Adolph Hitler and Osama Bin Laden all added enormously to the fear and misery in the world.

Conversely, Buddha, Jesus of Nazareth, Mohammad, Mahatma Gandhi, Nelson Mandela, Martin Luther King, Jr. and Mother Theresa all made contributions that were immensely disproportionate to their roles as individuals. They eased planetary suffering by demonstrating unconditional love and profound compassion for others. Their shining legacy continues to this day, even though some of the followers of Jesus and Mohammad, in particular, have tragically misinterpreted their masters' teachings.

Who's to say how significant your influence might be? As we keep reminding you, it's *your* choice. How will you live your life now that you are aware of your potential?

*Wait a minute, that's too heavy. What if I don't want all that responsibility? Or, even if I do want it, what if I'm not ready?*

You *always* have a choice. You can't do life wrong. If you choose to hold your light close, your influence will not be widely felt, though even a single candle lights the darkness. No one says you have to be a world leader, but it is important to understand that you are the author of your own script. You can write yourself in for a bit part, or for a lead role. Consider the following words, which we believe are some of the most inspiring in recent memory:

> "Our deepest fear is not that we are inadequate. Our deepest fear is that we are powerful beyond measure. It is our light, not our darkness, that most frightens us. We ask ourselves, Who am I to be brilliant, gorgeous, talented, fabulous? Actually, who are you not to be? You are a child of God. Your playing small doesn't serve the world. There's nothing enlightened about shrinking so that other people won't feel insecure around you. We are all meant to shine, as children do. We were born to make manifest the glory of God that is within us. It's not just in some of us; it's in everyone. And as we let our own light shine, we subconsciously give other people permission to do the same. As we're liberated from our own fear, our presence automatically liberates others."
>
> – From *A Return to Love*, by Marianne Williamson

# Way Beyond

(Acknowledging Rumi)

Out beyond
All we have known...
Way beyond

There is a field
Waiting in
Perfect silence

This field is pure potential
Sparkling brilliant
Sun-tossed color

Infinite possibilities
Dancing just
Out of reach…

While there are
No demons here
Fear's potential lies unaware

Next door to love's
Blissful destiny –
Which door will you

Knock on the next time
It's time to go beyond
Way beyond –

# 18 All the World's a Stage

All the world's a stage,
And all the men and women merely players.
They have their exits and their entrances,
And one man in his time plays many parts,
– *William Shakespeare*

*I understand the analogy you're using, though doesn't it trivialize the topics we're discussing? I mean, playing a part in a play is so different from real life.*

Maybe not as different as you think, and the analogy is certainly not intended to trivialize anything. We offer it only to illustrate certain profound similarities between what you experience as real life and the process of acting out a role. Let's explore this idea further. What would you say are some basic ingredients for an interesting story?

*Oh, that's easy. I love a good story. You need a compelling plot and some sub-plots. There should be an intriguing cast of characters, including a hero you can identify with, as well as a villain and several supporting actors. It should be set in an engaging time and place. It has to have an essential conflict, including a primary challenge the hero must overcome to save the day. It can't be easy, or it's boring. Heroes must be tested and even look as though they might fail, perhaps repeatedly, before finally succeeding. For me, that's what builds high drama.*

That's a good description. Let's look at your life and see if we can draw any comparisons. First, if you were fully cognizant of your omnipotent Divinity, no plot could ever provide you with much of a challenge. So, to make life a little more entertaining, the first thing you'd do would be to forget who you really are. Since, as God, you're infinitely powerful, it wouldn't be that great of a challenge for you to subdivide yourself and give each part amnesia, would it?

*Well, yeah, I guess that would be possible.*

OK, let's move on. Because of what we now understand is your self-induced amnesia, you would come into the world with no knowledge of who you really are. You would depend on others to help you learn about yourself and the things you need to know for survival. However, you would retain certain basic characteristics of your God essence, such as a fascination with all aspects of life and an appreciation for the inherent beauty of manifest creation.

In your initial awareness of existence in the physical plane, you quite naturally become the central character of your life. At some point after realizing that "you are," your exploration within this realm reveals natural limitations. Every hero is constrained in some way. Like Superman, every superhero is hindered by some version of lead or kryptonite. As you step into the hero role in your drama, you become acutely aware of your human frailties. These boundaries, as well as new possibilities, expand exponentially as civilization advances. Let's see how these boundaries and possibilities might play out.

# 19 Fire and Fear

> Courage is the fire that burns in the cold,
> dark room of fear and doubt that we live in.
> – *Anonymous*

Imagine your ancestors teaching their children all they knew about survival as they learned to thrive amongst the elements and deadly predators. Can you see how those who succeeded must have lived in constant awareness of the many hazards within their environment? Bravery and heroism were essential components of life. "Lions and tigers and bears, oh my…." But while there are indeed many fierce predators, the single most feared one down through the ages has always been your own species.

*That sounds terrifying. I can't imagine living in such a violent world.*

You can't? We weren't just speaking about some distant past; you're living in an intensely violent world right now. Just in the past 100 years, over 100 million people have been slaughtered in wars and genocidal orgies. Rwanda, Kosovo, Darfur; these are places where, just in the past decade, whole populations have been systematically decimated. Then there are the thousands of people who die every single day from extreme poverty.

And this isn't just about human-caused violence. Remember the Asian tsunami of December 2004, or the four hurricanes that hit Florida within six weeks that same summer? Even more recently, how about the monsoon that dumped 37 inches of rain on Mumbai, India in one day during July 2005? Not long after, hurricanes Katrina and

Rita brought devastation to huge swaths of the Gulf Coast and New Orleans. Then an enormously destructive earthquake struck Pakistan in October of 2005. The list goes on....

We especially want to caution you against taking stories of your ancestors' "miserable lives" too seriously. One of our teachings is that these stories have no basis in truth, they served only to justify the brutal conquest of indigenous peoples. While these genocidal invasions were done in the name of progress and religion, it was really about fear-driven greed.

The truth is, humans long ago learned to live quite well in many ways. It wasn't until the "leavers" were conquered by the "takers" that many lives became brutish and short.[21] In any event, we wish to emphasize that it was out of this constant observation of your environment that you began taking your first steps towards assuming a measure of control over it.

Take fire, for example. Archeologists have recently discovered clear evidence that your very distant ancestors, somewhere between 750,000 and 1.5 million years ago, were already proficient with its use. As you know, fire is a double-edged sword. It provides warmth, protection and the ability to cook, while in the blink of an eye it can also burn, maim or even kill. It can destroy forests, homes and entire cities, sending you fleeing for your life. Fire is a potent ally when used safely, such as in a hearth, stove or furnace. Used carelessly, perhaps malevolently, it is a deadly and implacable force. Fire does not require fear to be useful, though it absolutely requires respect. Most of you learn to fear fire early, by inadvertently burning yourselves on a stove, or perhaps with a match. In spite of the many dangers, though, fire remains endlessly fascinating.

*I love fireplaces. I can sit and stare into the flames for hours.*

Yes, the ritual of gazing raptly at flames and coals is burned deeply into your DNA. And over the millennia, you have used varying methods to instill respect for fire into your young. Some parents try to protect their children from burning themselves, while failing to teach about the potentially fatal consequences of "playing with fire." Others allow their kids to explore their environment, including burning themselves, as a quick and reasonably sure method of teaching them that fire is dangerous.

Extending this analogy, some of you continue to "teach" by instilling fear in general. You use corporal punishment, humiliation, screaming and other manifestations of rage in order to force children immediately to do what they're told. In these and many other ways you make them "wrong" when they make choices that don't meet with your approval. Some parents, with a shrug of their shoulders, even dismiss or laugh off actions that could result in harm or even death.

*It sounds as though instilling fear or letting children learn through hurting themselves are the only parenting choices you see. Isn't there a more positive, proactive approach?*

Of course there is. The wisdom to raise healthy, curious, creative and caring children is readily available. We direct you to the *Positive Discipline* series by Jane Nelsen. She has by far the most loving, respectful, consciouas approach to parenting we've ever come across.

In order to maintain its control, your culture perpetuates an authoritarian structure designed to teach children what you subjectively consider to be right and wrong, rather than how to make accountable choices on their own. You instill in them a story that they are fundamentally less than you are, using your greater size and strength to reinforce that teaching. In the long run, this doesn't really make your children safer, though you may have convinced yourself otherwise.

You've simply confused control with teaching your children to think, as well as act, in ways that ensure their safety, especially when you aren't around to both monitor and manage their behavior.

You have created social environments for your children wherein pecking orders are quickly established and maintained, based largely on physical strength and attractiveness. You support the display of images that inform them in countless ways that they will never be as beautiful or handsome, as happy or carefree, as cool or accepted as the computer-enhanced supermodels shown on TV or in magazines. Never, that is, unless they literally buy into whatever those models are selling. By their 18th birthday, they have seen, on average, well over a million advertising impressions. These images have been carefully crafted by experts trained to appeal to their deeply ingrained sense of lack as well as their desire to conform to your incredibly narrow standards of sexual attractiveness.

*I know I've fallen victim to this many times. Quite often, after purchasing something, I experience buyer's remorse. I wonder, what could I have been thinking?*

That's it exactly! You are not a victim here, you're an active participant. You decided to purchase that item you neither needed nor wanted. You can see that your culture has created an amazingly effective system for teaching your children about fear, lack and limitations. Nearly all of you have been raised to feel as though you are simply not good enough, but that maybe, just maybe, if you acquire enough stuff, no one will notice. The mighty marketing machine relentlessly drowns you in advertising, and you continue to binge-buy even at the expense of your families, society and the environment. In this never-ending quest to get what you think you need so that you can "measure up," the basic elements of all the plots and subplots in this drama are in place.

As for your cast of characters, you never seem to have a shortage. You become the protagonist of your story through your imagination-fueled ego, while fears, the need for acceptance and your quest for conformity set boundaries on your originality. Reaching for this impossible goal of constantly being the hero in your story, you're faced with the cultural baggage that you're not good enough "To dream the impossible dream." Many people elevate others, especially movie, music and sports stars, to the role of a hero. Upon closer inspection, though, they also turn out to be entirely human, with feet of clay.

Failing to meet the impossible expectations you've set up, you create scapegoats to serve as the villains in your play. After all, you have to blame someone when the world fails to bow at your feet. The villain might be your boss, your spouse, your parents, the government, virtually anyone or anything in your life will do. This process is known as "projection,"[22] where we project onto another those parts of ourselves which we most dislike, and often disown, in ourselves.

As an example, let's say that you have an issue with owning your own anger (and if this hits close to the mark, it's entirely intentional. Disowning anger is one of the most common traits of humanity). When you disown your anger, you'll experience lots of angry people showing up in your life, blowing off volcanos of emotion for no apparent reason. After all, you're an innocent victim, right? Then, at some point, you "discover" and own your anger. Suddenly (or so it seems) most of the angry people who had been making your life a living hell seem to vanish. All of the angry people in your life don't really go away, it's just that you've stopped projecting your anger on them, so they're no longer in reaction to you. It may seem like magic, but it's really just common sense.

For many of you, failing to achieve goals engenders the need to set the responsibility outside of your domain, thus creating victim consciousness. Out of your desperation, you need to make someone or something else wrong, because taking personal responsibility feels like failure, and you have been taught that failing is for losers. All the while, at least on a subconscious level, you intuitively know it's your own actions that are the cause.

*I hate it when I fail. Sometimes I do feel like a loser. Are you saying that failing doesn't make us losers?*

Absolutely. Judging an experience to be a failure is a choice. And as we've been saying, whenever you recognize a choice point, you have the opportunity to tell yourself another story. Thomas Edison, when asked by a reporter how it felt to have failed for so long to come up with results for a project he was working on, replied, "Results! Why, man, I have gotten a lot of results. I know several thousand things that won't work."

It's all good. Failure, success, in the long run it hardly matters, except for what you make it mean. We are reminded of the timeless quote, "The person who dies with the most toys … is still dead!" Most of you are not remembered for either the quality *or* quantity of your toys, but rather how much love you shared when you were alive.

## Great Beacons

Oh you invincible bearers
Of unbearable sorrow

You great beacons
Of invincible heartlight

Purveyors of Blessings and all
Life can bestow

Gentle hands caressing hearts
In the darkest hour

Oh you heralds of the dawn
Singing sweetly of life

Always totally available
Never a bit intrusive

The Friend who never fails
To reflect the truth of who we are

Oh Angels of light
Come to love us Home

Right here, right now
Oh you incandescent Beings

Sing to us of Home
Sing us Home now…

# 20 God-As-Us

> Unity consciousness is a state of enlightenment where we pierce the mask of illusion which creates separation and fragmentation. Behind the appearance of separation is one unified field of wholeness. Here the seer and the scenery are one.
>
> – *Deepak Chopra*

Let us continue with our examination of the elements of a good drama. Most of you don't consider the places where you live and work to be exotic, or the time in which you live to be particularly exciting. You use television to stimulate your imagination to the point where the line between personal and vicarious experience becomes blurred. The ever-increasing pace at which your society moves gives little time to experience the exotic, even while living in the midst of it.

You have become so skilled at creating conflict that it's often quite abundant in your life. Of course, since you're still God (even though you've forgotten), you are powerful creators and defenders of the challenges and limitations you bring into your life. You are so thoroughly invested in your stories of fear, lack and victim consciousness that even the *thought* of letting them go can feel threatening. Hanging on to these stories is how you create maximum conflict. As long as you're lost in these stories, you unerringly continue to manifest high drama. Remember, God-As-Us adores a good story.

*Now I'm confused. You said earlier that God doesn't want us to suffer, that our pain is God's pain. Then you said that God loves a good story, and this apparently requires the high drama that comes from watching our attempts to overcome some hurt or hardship. Which is it?*

Both. This dance between not wanting us to suffer and loving a good story is another example of duality playing itself out. Your question assumes that God is watching everything like an owner of a sports franchise, sitting above the fray in a luxurious box seat. From our perspective, nothing could be further from the truth. God-As-Us is the stage, the playwright and every character. You are not puppets, play-acting for God's amusement. You are nothing less than God in human form!

Yes, God loves a good story, and as we've already discussed, a good story requires certain things. You need a plot that includes good guys, bad guys and the chance to become part of a small band fighting against hopeless odds. These components have long formed the core of your favorite stories, which is why you keep living them out! It's in this revelatory moment of awareness, and *only* in this moment, that you can choose to write a new story. Actually, millions of you already have. That is what this book, as well as so many others, is all about.

*So... **anything** that pleases us also pleases God? If that's so, then why not live a totally hedonistic life, moving from one pleasure to the next? Come to think of it, if the now moment is all we ever have, then maybe I should just live for this moment and have as much fun as possible right now, without regard for consequences. Maybe I should just eat, drink and be merry!*

That's certainly one way to look at it, and since you're God and you can't do it wrong, you can run with that perspective if it serves you. You wouldn't be alone, for heaven's sake.

*Wow, that's not the answer I expected!*

What did you expect?

*Some sort of moral sanction on that kind of behavior, I suppose. Frankly, I'm disappointed and more than a little confused by your answer.*

Moral sanctions are nothing more or less than someone else's judgments. As to your disappointment, that's your judgment.

*So… are you saying it's perfectly all right for anyone to go out and just take what they want? Raping, pillaging, plundering and general mayhem are fine, just because it pleases them?*

Would *you* find that behavior pleasing?

*I've never even considered acting like that, but it must appeal to some people or they wouldn't do it. But wait a minute, that's crazy! I can't believe I'm having a dialog with my higher self in which you seem to be telling me I can forget all the rules and live for the moment. This is getting way too weird!*

We do not recall telling you to forget all the rules and live for the moment. Actually, we have been very clear that it's not our role to tell you how to act, or even to presume that we know what you should or should not do. However, you might find it useful to notice that there is a very big difference between living *for* the moment and living *in* the moment. Whatever choices you make are just that, *your* choices. And it is those choices, along with the consequences they create, that constitute the context in which this game is played. Without the ability to make choices, there is no game at all.

*Hold it. I asked you about eating, drinking and being merry. What is all this about living for or living in the moment?*

Please bear with us, we're getting there. But first, let's take a few steps back so we can see a larger picture. As humans, you instinctively move away from perceived pain towards perceived pleasure. This is a hardwired reaction common to virtually all life, though there are exceptions, especially when it comes to protecting your young. In each moment, you can either choose to move *away* from pain and fear, or move *towards* love, peace, serenity and joy. The choice of moving *towards* love as opposed to moving *away* from fear is striking. Love and fear are two poles in your emotional life. You tend to ping-pong unconsciously between them until you wake up and realize you actually have a choice.

Given that, one who lives *for* the moment is forever seeking instant gratification. Why? Because deep down, that person holds a belief that they are either incapable or unworthy of achieving true joy and fulfillment in their lives. Hedonists tend to ignore consequences, seeking pleasure at the expense of personal responsibility. They attempt to fill the aching hole in their hearts with sensory overload, though this ultimately proves to be a futile exercise. In the end, the ache remains, intensified by the realization that it is impossible to fill this hole with mindless self-indulgence. They have succeeded only in becoming trapped by their own stories.

In contrast, those who live *in* the moment recognize the significance of consequences. They choose to live each moment consistent with the belief that they deserve true joy in their lives as well as fulfilling their purpose for being. They see themselves as powerful, because they are fully accountable for their choices and the ensuing consequences. This moment is a snapshot, one frame in the film of their lives, and they realize that they are the director as well as the screenwriter. They treasure each frame, because they know that this film is composed of single now moments. Each now moment, each frame, is a reflection of the quality of their choices, accumulating in a film representing their lives.

*OK, now I see the difference. It's clear to me that my choice is to live in the moment. I just don't see how I can do this all the time.*

We honor your choice, dear one. These are the real challenges. Not only to wake up and remember who you are, realizing that it's all an elaborate play, but also to *stay* awake. When you are able to grok this truth, you come to have a sense of peace about the outcome of your endeavors. While you will still strive to do your best, in this remembering you recognize that, ultimately, you are God. In that moment you know that your life is both transitory *and* eternal, and that your real source of power always is, as it always has been, your ability to make conscious choices as you write the story of your life.

# 21 Fear and Love

Love brings forth that which is unlike itself
to be healed.

– *Judith Guggenheim*

*OK, I think I've got it. I understand the analogy of life as a Great Passion Play, but there's one thing that still doesn't make sense. If we're God, making it all up, why make it so hard on ourselves? If we really have a choice, why not make it easy? Why all the struggle, fear and suffering that seem to pervade most people's lives?*

Simply because most people have no idea that choices are available. Remember, one of the most challenging aspects of taking responsibility for your life is realizing that other choices have been available all along. The only choice many of you have made is to give your power away. It could be in favor of other people's opinions – whether in the context of your schools, churches, political parties, the government or even your friends, the end result is the same – you set yourselves up as victims. Media outlets, including newspapers, magazines, TV, movies, popular music and endless advertising, are the primary conduits of most of these messages. They tell you what to desire, how to look, to act and even what to feel, all in the guise of making your lives better.

We are reminded of the 40-year-old lyrics from the classic "Satisfaction," by the Rolling Stones: "When I'm watching my TV/and that man comes on and tells me/how white my shirts can be/but he can't be a man 'cause he doesn't smoke/the same cigarettes as me."

Notice the subliminal message that you aren't good enough (let alone perfect) as you are. What is also happening, though, is that you are being encouraged to distract yourself from feeling powerless. After all, as long as you can make a choice for a new house, car, or any of the myriad other things you trade your life force for, it does seem as though you are manifesting power. In contrast, Gary Zukav, in his excellent book *Seat of the Soul*, defines authentic power as "The alignment of the personality with the soul." Do you see the immense difference between these two ways of feeling powerful?

*Yes, it's like night and day.*

Understanding the distinction is a crucial step for you to take towards claiming your own authentic power. Our deepest desire is for you to grok, so profoundly you hold it at a cellular level, that you are totally in control of your life. You are a sovereign being, an awesome spark of God/Goddess. Every good thing in the world, including clean, wholesome food to eat; a warm, dry home; loving, supportive family and friends; feeling safe and, in truth, all you desire, are absolutely your birthright. The bottom line is that you *are* good enough. You are truly worthy of love, respect and honor, simply because you, as well as *everyone* on this planet, are precious sparks of God-As-Us.

*But that doesn't answer my question. Even if we, as humans, are clueless about our birthright and all that we deserve, why didn't we, as God, design the play to be an easier experience?*

Because the game you agreed to play was to see how far you could take the illusion of separation, how alone, scared, isolated and separate you could allow yourselves to feel, and *still* find your way Home again. Actually, you're all performing at Oscar-winning levels. You get into your parts so thoroughly you completely forget about who you really are. Talk about the ultimate in method acting – what an incredible rush!

*That's certainly a different perspective. At some point I might even come to think of it as refreshing, but for now the question remains; why make it so hard to remember who we really are?*

Simply because, as God, any choice other than to play fully is inconceivable. Think about it. Have you ever played a game that seemed too easy? How was it for you to play that game?

*Well, I got bored and stopped playing.*

Exactly! That's why you created this game the way you did, so each spark of God/Goddess can choose to live fully within the context of the story. Imagine for a moment that you're on stage performing. Wouldn't it be incredibly distracting to have someone in the audience shouting, "It's just a play! Don't take it seriously!" Likewise, if you were in the audience really getting into the play, wouldn't you be extremely annoyed if the person sitting next to you kept leaning over and whispering, "It's just a play. Don't get lost in it."

*I must admit you have a point. But if our purpose for existing as humans is to continually play our hearts out, why does anyone ever choose to wake up?*

Because that's part of the game too. Those of you choosing to wake up to the realization that you are God/Goddess in form are still part of the game. You're just more conscious of what's going on, and so are able to choose less suffering.

*I find myself rather surprised to be saying it, but this is starting to make sense. I feel strangely satisfied, sort of like when I'm fiddling with a pair of binoculars and the view suddenly comes into focus. Just so I'm sure I understand, may we return to an earlier statement you made? You said that fear and love are nexus points around which duality revolves. Would you please tell me more about what that means?*

Yes, gladly. We are delighted that this is beginning to make sense to you. As for love and fear, remember that within the Great Passion Play, you each have your own perspective, based on your individual stories. It's through these stories that you ultimately determine the meaning of your life. Within this context, there are critical turning points when you make fundamental choices about whether to see the world through the eyes of fear or love.

Fear-Based Consciousness (FBC) sees danger everywhere. FBC is rooted in a static, zero-sum game, where the totality of all things is finite. Whether tangible, such as money and possessions, or intangible, such as joy and love, anyone's gain always must be balanced by someone else's loss. This underlying assumption of lack fuels a perpetual victim mentality.

In contrast to FBC, Love-Based Consciousness (LBC) comes from a perspective of infinite abundance. It sees the universe as truly expansive, in a way that allows for continuous creativity. While there may, at times, appear to be a shortage of material things, LBC sustains the creative process, encouraging innovative ways to manifest abundance. By enlisting our infinitely productive potential as conscious co-creators, it's possible to transform what is less useful into what is more useful, without doing so at the expense of people or the environment.

Over the course of a lifetime, nearly all people exhibit behavior consistent with both LBC and FBC, though most usually live from a core perspective of one or the other. People who live in FBC are generally unaware that this is where they are coming from. Whether aware or not, it remains the foundation of their stories, and therefore their lives.

If you were to select some people at random, and define LBC and FBC for them, most would fervently assure you that they are in the LBC camp, even passionately arguing with you to prove it. This, in itself, can be a strong indication that they do indeed come from fear.

One truly living in LBC would just as passionately desire to explore their reality and reveal their truth, rather than blindly defend their position. They would see someone else's judgment as just that, a judgment, and not take it personally.

*That's easy for you to say. But when someone lays their trip on me and they're obviously full of it, I can't just let it stand.*

Well, actually you could. It's a choice. If you wish to escalate conflict, by all means respond, preferably with righteous indignation. That's pretty much guaranteed to get the sparks flying. Just notice that at the root of your anger lies fear.

The sad truth is that the majority of humans alive today are grounded in FBC, which in no way implies that love doesn't touch their lives, or that they aren't nice people. It is simply that those who come from FBC have a more limited awareness of the infinite presence of love. On the other hand, those living in LBC are aware that it is infinitely expansive, encompassing many more of the myriad possibilities of love's full expression.

LBC simply leaves no room for FBC to foster negativity. Nearly everyone, at some level, longs for LBC but fails to achieve it, especially on a consistent basis. Why? Because those who are limited by a story of lack see themselves as victims, believing it is someone else's responsibility to initiate love. Terrified of rejection, they dare not open their hearts.

Not being able to see that there is indeed enough love is a vicious cycle. Love, by its very nature, can only be given, with no assurance it will be returned. Everyone has experienced rejection and the pain it brings, but pain, as we've seen earlier, is merely feedback. Like every other experience in your life, you have the choice to interpret it however you wish.

One choice is to believe that the pain of rejection means you should never risk reaching out to others. You equate rejection with not being good enough, that you are not worthy of love. Another choice holds that the person rejecting you was simply unable to receive the love you offered, that their rejection isn't about you, it's about them.

It is important here to recognize that you *always* have choices. Please remember that the core choice you make in each moment, about whether you will come from LBC or FBC, literally *creates* your reality. You rarely, if ever, directly experience events, only your interpretations of them as they pass through the filters of your beliefs.

# 22 Making Stuff Up (MSU)

Turn your wounds into wisdom.
– *Oprah Winfrey*

*Are you saying that objective reality doesn't really matter? That the events of our lives, even the major ones, are less important than the meaning we choose to give them?*

To be quite explicit, we are saying that outside of your stories, events have no meaning for you whatsoever. The events of your life are the "isness" we've spoken so much about, while *how you are* with the "isness" is the key to experiencing life as suffering or bliss.

Let us take this idea a bit further. There is a perspective called Making Stuff Up (MSU). It refers to the way many people, as they awaken from the stories of fear and lack that so deeply permeate your culture, consciously begin creating their moment-to-moment experience. On the surface, MSU might sound like a way of avoiding reality, though actually it's a way of empowering yourself by redefining your experience of it. No matter what happens outside of your sphere of influence in the world, you always have the freedom to determine what you will allow events to mean. Grokking MSU gives you the power to make choices. It's up to you to decide in which direction, towards fear or towards love, you will go.

For example, take a moment to remember an event that you regard as a negative turning point in your life, a victim story in which you felt thoroughly taken advantage of. Got it?

*Oh, yeah, I've got a doosey! I remember a time when....*

Perfect! Just hold that thought. Now, close your eyes and bring the event into focus. How did it start? Recreate as many details as you can. Did it happen quickly, or over a period of time? Remember how you felt. Were you hurt, disappointed, disillusioned, angry, all of the above? Take a few moments to relive the story, being sure to cast yourself as the innocent victim. Who was the villain? Now, write it down. Capture every nuance, making sure that anyone reading it (no one will, this is for your eyes only) would clearly understand what a raw deal you got.

*Wow, I'm surprised at how vivid that memory still is. I thought I'd let that go a long time ago. I can't believe how naïve I was.*

Good job. Now, take another piece of paper and rewrite the same story, but this time tell it from the perspective of full accountability. Do not cast anyone, including yourself, as either the victim or the villain. This is not about blame, but rather about accounting for the choices you made before, during and after the event.

After you have finished rewriting your story, let's take it to the next level. Look at the choices you made, and consider some of the other options that were available to you. It is critical that you be gentle with yourself. This inquiry is about seeing possibilities you might not have noticed before. Could you have made different choices, either before or during the event, which would have produced different results? We are not suggesting that any of your choices were wrong, simply offering an exploration of some alternatives.

How are you doing? Is this exercise working for you?

*Yes, though I'm feeling a lot of blame at every turn of the events in my story. I've always felt like such a victim, and now I realize that what this person did wasn't even about me. This exercise helped me see that I could have made different choices. It's embarrassing!*

We deeply appreciate how you might feel that way. While it is common to feel embarrassed, we wish to point out that this feeling is also a choice. When you begin to shift from FBC into LBC, grokking that you have, and have always had, many choices, you may feel as though you have previously made many poor decisions. For this very reason, many people actively resist accepting responsibility for their experiences. Your identity becomes so wrapped up in victim consciousness that letting go of it can feel like death itself.

This issue of taking responsibility for all past choices and their consequences is why so many people who are on a healing path experience such intense resistance from the ego. Fueled by their ego's terror of being "found out," their inner dialogue creates a life filled with chaos in order to distract them from healing into LBC. Some version of, "I'm wounded, therefore I am," echoes incessantly in the ego's mind chatter.

One of the teachings we bring is that, once the ego fully understands that it will not be punished for past choices, it can actually become a trusted and important ally in this amazing journey called life. Endless adventures await those who are willing to let go of FBC and embrace LBC, and the ego can definitely come along for the ride.

For now, let's look specifically at the choices you made after the event about which you just wrote. How did you choose to interpret this episode in your life? Did you allow it to feed your sense of victim consciousness? Did you harbor resentments? Do you still? Do the memories of this event, and your unresolved feelings about it, continue to have an impact on your life? Does reliving some portion of this experience spill out on those around you, poisoning existing relationships and contaminating new ones? Are you, in effect, carrying around a balloon full of unfelt emotions that seems about to burst?

*Now that you mention it, I feel quite sad. I really thought I'd put all that behind me, but clearly I haven't. I'm still holding on to old grievances.*

We're not surprised. Please realize that from this moment on you have the ability to choose what you will make this event mean. If you choose to stop feeding the memory it must wither, releasing any remaining hold it may have. The key to this healing process is MSU, using its power to redefine the meaning you give your history. Choose love over fear. In its highest, most cleansing form, love always includes the choice to forgive everyone towards whom you have been carrying a grudge, including yourself. Remember to look for the gifts in each experience, especially in those you have tried the hardest to forget.

*I feel as though a yawning chasm has opened in the middle of who I thought I was. I feel terrified and excited all at once.*

Wonderful! You are making excellent progress. If you are not quite ready to give up your negative feelings, simply begin to consider the possibility. Imagine taking a backpack and tossing into it as many bricks as it would take to build a wall of isolation and mistrust. You will either need a really large backpack, or it'll be a small wall, and for the purposes of this exercise, either one is fine. Write a word or two on each brick representing feelings in your balloon that no longer serve you. Carry the backpack everywhere. How long will you choose to haul around all those bricks? Whenever you are ready, take out a brick or two and notice how much lighter you feel.

When the backpack is empty, we are sure you will grok LBC on a much deeper level. You will become aware that the major difference between FBC and LBC is that FBC is about *taking*, while LBC is about *giving*. Fear never trusts that there is enough, so it takes before someone else does. Love is aware of the fundamental law that God-As-Us wove into the fabric of the universe; the more love you give, the more you become aware of its infinite abundance.

## Possibilities

Possibilities saunter casually past my awareness
Like autumn leaves full of color and spice,

Crisp and deceased, reminders of
Death's relentless illusion

We bury our heads in the fetid loam
Of our fevered imaginations,

Forever seeking more…
Toys, money, status, power,

Indoctrinated by fear-based programming
To stay lost and safe in our comfortable cells

While outside the wilderness calls
On the west wind, moon glinting

Mystery over the far horizon,
Undiscovered country at our feet

We kneel down and spill our broken tears
Onto the bosom of our Mother,

More terrified of living
Than of death –

# 23 Quan Yin, the Goddess of Mercy, Compassion and Forgiveness

Mercy means that more assistance is given through love than merit earned.

– *Quan Yin*

My message is the practice of compassion, love and kindness. Compassion can be put into practice if one recognizes the fact that every human being is a member of humanity and the human family regardless of differences in religion, culture, color and creed. Deep down there is no difference.

– *Dalai Lama*

Forgiveness is the answer to a dream of a miracle ... by which what is broken is made whole again ... what is soiled is again made clean.

– *Dag Hammarskjold*

*I can't believe all those feelings I've been carrying around. My back seems about to break! I now see what you mean by my stories creating my experience, and I feel like an idiot for creating all this suffering in my life. I have a whole new appreciation for the saying, "Ignorance is bliss."*

Your feelings are quite understandable, especially in the context of your old stories. Just notice that your judgments are the cause of your suffering, and remember that you have many choices. In this moment, for example, you can choose mercy, compassion and forgiveness. We have often found it useful to invoke the legend of Quan Yin, an ancient Chinese Buddhist Goddess who carries the Divine Mother aspect of Buddhism and embodies the concept of the Bodhisattva. A Bodhisattva is an enlightened being, one who has become liberated from pain-filled stories of birth, death, and rebirth. These enlightened beings vow to remain in the earthly realms until all others have completed their own enlightenment. Consider invoking her gift of unconditional love right now. As you open your heart to the truth that you have always been doing the best you can within the context of your stories, forgive yourself. As Gandhi said, "The weak can never forgive. Forgiveness is the attribute of the strong."

*That may be easy for him to say, but I've been such a fool!*

Not really. You have been God pretending not to be. Now you are awakening. As your eyes and heart open, many of the stories that used to enthrall you will no longer be so entertaining. Notice, though, how easy it can be to fall back into the core story of not being good enough.

*So, what can I do to let go of these harsh criticisms? I can't even seem to think clearly.*

Simply return to your breath and consciously choose peace. You have been on quite a journey, and as with any journey, sometimes it's best to stop and rest. As you breathe, imagine someone in your life who has loved you just the way you are. As you breathe this love into your heart, feel your heart expand with joy. This unconditional, infinite love, including the mercy, compassion and forgiveness of Quan Yin, is always available, only one choice away. You deserve this love, which heals, nurtures and supports your entire being. With sweet tenderness, notice your breathing deepen, your heart slow, and feel yourself become present. You can use this simple technique any time you notice yourself diving into fear.

*Whew! That was intense. I'm amazed at how vicious my own thoughts became, and how crazy I began to feel. What was that all about?*

Really? Amazed? You've never heard those voices before, never felt those feelings, that siren call of adrenaline?

*Well ... now that you mention it. That's what this has all been leading up to, hasn't it? Getting me to notice how I distract myself from my feelings with the adrenaline rushes I create out of my fear-based stories. That's how I sabotage myself. It's an endless feedback loop!*

It's only endless as long as you don't change the channel. Return to your breath, to Quan Yin, to choosing mercy. Mercy is simply a disposition to be kind and forgiving. Then choose compassion, which is the deep awareness of the suffering of another coupled with the desire to relieve it. In this case, your higher self (who you really are) is choosing compassion for that part of you who has been lost in your stories of fear and lack. Finally, choose forgiveness, which is the act of pardoning a mistake or offense, for others as well as yourself.

Forgiving is not about anyone else. It's a personal statement that you are committed to love, and a powerful declaration that you are about giving. It comes from a profound understanding of the Truth of who you really are, and that you're always doing the best you can, given your perspective at the time. This is not to say that what others do is necessarily OK; it may not be at all. But we are saying that forgiveness is the ability to see that people lost in FBC are making the best choices they are capable of in that moment, even when those choices wind up hurting themselves and others.

You need to separate their behavior from who they really are, and deeply grok that their wounding of others springs directly out of their own pain, and is not some capricious or malevolent act of evil. In short, people lost in fear do what they think is best for their own self-preservation. They are not necessarily *trying* to hurt you; you're simply collateral damage. One analogy is that of the cat who scratches your arm as it jumps. It's not trying to scratch you, it's just trying to get down.

*Wow, staying that conscious when I'm flailing about in fear feels like a lot to ask.*

We ask only for you to love and respect yourself as the Divine Blessing you are. Give yourself the gift of loving kindness.

*That's easy for you to say. You don't seem affected by adrenaline at all.*

Indeed we are not. You, however, are as addicted to adrenaline as anyone else. After all, it is an essential element of the Great Passion Play. Our teaching is that love gives you at least as big a thrill as fear ever could, and it also feels *way* better.

# 24 The Primal Emotions of Fear and Panic

The most potent weapon in the hands of the oppressor is the mind of the oppressed.
– *Steven Biko*

You truly live in a miraculous world filled with life's blessings, including the exquisite ecstasy of unconditional love. Yet this world can appear frightening, even terrifying. There is no doubt that you have often wrestled with your fears. You may even be searching for ways to alleviate them, knowing how debilitating they can become when you surrender to them. On a planetary level, the consequences of bowing to the tyranny of fear results in the "isness" you face today. War, terrorism, global warming, rampant hunger, tsunamis, earthquakes, hurricanes and rapidly mutating diseases can all seem overwhelming, even in the midst of astonishing abundance.

*Our planet certainly does seem to operate out of Fear-Based-Consciousness, as you put it, though how could we continue living in such a dangerous world, or even get anything accomplished, if we didn't know fear?*

We certainly agree that fear, including the fear of failure, is a deeply ingrained neuronal pathway. Your planetary culture has set you up to fear failure. For your world to function as it does, those in power *need* you to live in fear. Please understand this; fear does *not* keep you safe. Fear simply keeps you stuck in the shadows of your potential.

Political will, backed by the very real threat of incarceration and bodily harm, is enforced by the police and military. The media incessantly and hysterically floods your senses with stories of war, killers, rapists, disasters and diseases such as HIV, Ebola, avian flu and cancer, along with whatever might be the threat du jour. Why? Because the truth is, it's incredibly effective in maintaining the status quo of Fear-Based-Consciousness, which allows those in power to remain there. As long as the population is kept in fear, you're relatively easy to control. Additionally, hooking you on sensationalized stories creates a built-in audience for the endless commercial messages the media feeds on.

It's important to remember that those in power are run by fear as well. Not only those fears you hold in common, but also the fear that they will lose their power and may be held accountable for any abuse of it. Perhaps their deepest fear is that, knowing in their heart of hearts that abusing power is fundamentally out of alignment with honor, respect and loving kindness, they will have their power not only stripped away but also used against them. And so, set against the great sweep of history, popular uprisings and revolutions unfold, the oppressed wresting control from their oppressors, only to have this sad cycle play out, like a broken record, again and again.

*How can I hold this truth in my consciousness and not get lost in rage over the way things are?*

Allow your compassionate heart to open and you will see the power mongers for who they really are, children of God/Goddess who are just as lost in fear as those they oppress. Seeing this clearly may be a significant challenge as you look at many of your world leaders, perhaps especially so when looking at those in your own country. It is important, however, to maintain your compassion while considering this, as any negativity you hold towards another affects you as well. FBC thrives when nourished by negativity, while LBC promotes compassion and unity. We remind you of these truths so that, as we discuss fear and adrenaline, we may be on the same page.

*Yes, I vividly remember what you said earlier about LBC and FBC.*

Excellent. You see, fear is encoded in your DNA. You actually have proof of this from the laboratory. Using a relatively new technology called functional Magnetic Resonance Imaging, or fMRI, which allows brain functioning to be imaged in real time, researchers have recently traced several primal emotions to the limbic system of the brain, specifically the amygdala.[23] Among them are rage (fight), panic (flight), separation anxiety, lust and seeking.

In this case, seeking refers to the deeply ingrained behavior that causes many living creatures to, in effect, see what's over the next hill. Mice, when wired up to have their seeking neuronal pathways stimulated, will, even when hungry, ignore food that's placed in front of them, stand up on their hind legs and sniff around for new opportunities.

These instinctual drives form some of your deepest, most basic emotions. It is important to note that all of these drives have a powerful association with survival. We find it fascinating that those in control (often white men, oddly enough), have turned all of these primal drives against the rest of you, making you wrong, even sinners, for having these feelings. It is not these emotions, in and of themselves, that creates your suffering. Rather, it's that they are misunderstood and taken as signs that you are unworthy, even bad or evil people. Nothing could be further from the truth.

It is crucial for you to understand the makeup of your body in order to gain some measure of mastery over these emotions (which can also be thought of as instincts, or drives), that are hardwired into your

DNA. They exist to help you survive, at all costs, at least long enough to reproduce. For the purposes of our discussion, we will focus here on rage and panic, and how they work within you.

Rage can be a useful emotion if harm threatens you or your family. Panic can also be useful if you need to move quickly out of harm's way. What rage and panic have in common is a powerful surge of the hormone called adrenaline, which in the blink of an eye can energize the body so that it can either fight or take flight. Since ultimately you are Divine sparks of God/Goddess, you are essentially immortal. The body, however, is most definitely not. This dichotomy of distractions is the crux of this Great Passion Play, what makes life so fascinating and profoundly compelling.

*While I feel somewhat reassured to hear that I am immortal, I'm still terrified of dying. How do I deal with that?*

Just breathe into your fear, and remember, as Robert Heller said, "Fear is excitement without breath." You can hold on to your story that death is to be feared, or you can choose a new one that holds death as a grand journey into the frontiers of consciousness. We're reminded of the line in *Peter Pan*, with the tide rising up the rock in the lagoon where Peter and Wendy are stranded. All looks lost, and Peter says, "To die will be an awfully big adventure." No matter which story you choose, death is still inevitable. For now, just know that, in the words of Emmanuel,[24] the being Pat Rodegast channels, "Death is *absolutely* safe."

# The News

I don't want to watch the news tonight
I already know that things aren't right –

Somewhere people are killing each other
Family against family, brother against brother,

And some damn freak who calls himself an Earl
Has raped his 28th nine-year-old girl –

I know the country is deeper in debt
And somebody's eaten the family pet,

Some fool's spilled radioactive oil
And opened another pus-filled boil

In the polluted soil of our Mother planet,
God damn it –

Someone else just lost a friend
And countless lives came to an end

Before they could get back to the dreams
They'd set aside in mid-stream

To follow the ubiquitous evening news
And sit on the ancient wooden pews,

Listening as life is explained in detail
So that no one can possibly fail

To understand the do's and don'ts
And who it is you will or won't

Be in this ordered life we lead –
By the way, my inner voice intercedes,

It would never do to plead your case,
Guilt is written all over your face

And, after all, I've made it clear
That all these things you hold so dear

Are nothing to me, no more than a flea
Surfing the foam on a windswept sea

Or a leaf shredding in the teeth of a gale…
No, sorry, my inner voice said. No sale.

Besides, there's a life that waits for you
Once you blow off the news and discover the truth

Beyond the waking dream you've always known
And the nightmares that make you moan –

There's a wounded child hiding deep inside,
One who plays in the sun and chases the tide,

Who wriggles all over at a tender touch,
Knowing that nothing else means as much

As retaking the time we thought we had lost
Before we stopped to reckon the cost –

Now I have a new life I'm creating,
And the only news I watch is of my own making –

# 25 Fear and the Siren Call of Adrenaline

> When you have good thoughts, happy thoughts, it's a completely different set of chemicals than when you're feeling angry or hopeless.
>
> – *Dr. Daniel Amen*

Your fear of dying can easily cause panic, and, in a heartbeat, flood your body with adrenaline. There is no thought, no consideration at all in this process. When a threat is imminent, your body's reaction must be instantaneous. When your ancestors walked through a forest and heard a sudden rustle in the bushes, they didn't have the luxury of pondering what may have made the noise. They needed to be elsewhere more or less instantly, or you wouldn't be here now. The ability to jump several feet straight up into the air (now an Olympic sport known as the high jump), then grab a tree branch and scramble to safety, was a necessity rather than an option.

Though the saber-tooth tiger is no longer with you, there are still times when you may find yourself in need of expeditiously extricating yourself from the path of that seemingly malevolent taxi. Although those instincts are still very much a part of who you are, it is clear that immediate physical danger is not a common experience in the developed world, unless you deliberately seek it out. Since virtually everyone develops an intense adrenaline addiction while still in the womb, you have found endless ways to feed this "jones," regardless of perceived external dangers.

In this Great Passion Play, however, many millions of you find yourselves in war zones, faced with catastrophic natural disasters, or simply trying to get home through the chaos of a traffic-choked freeway. In these cases, fear or panic has a clear and present source. In modern society, there are a myriad of ways to get an adrenaline fix, many of them far more subtle than the ones already listed. Some of you deliberately seek out adventures such as skydiving, hurtling down a ski slope, driving recklessly or watching horror movies, all of which allow you to suckle at adrenaline's demanding breast.

So that we may delve more deeply into the connection between fear and adrenaline, would you please share what it is, then, that you fear?

*That's easy. Like I said, I fear death! And naturally, we have to be aware of danger. Everyone knows that, it's just common sense. Though I think I now understand why you're making such a big deal out of adrenaline, I'm still not sure what it has to do with rage and all the rest?*

Well, in addition to whatever physical dangers still exist in everyday life, you are taught to fear whatever those in power decide is expedient at the time. The deliberate creation of these fears is designed to keep you in line and endlessly consuming. For many of you, your greatest fears include not being cool, not looking just right, losing a job, losing face, divorce, humiliation, growing older and much, much more. Notice how shame lives at the root of all of these fears. The central theme here is that you *should* avoid these experiences at all costs. At the same time, your culture is profoundly addicted to the adrenaline rush that fear brings. If you are truly to gain mastery over fear, it's imperative that you come to a deep appreciation of the siren call of adrenaline.

*I feel somewhat embarrassed to say that I recognize a few of these scenarios from my own life. Are you saying I'm addicted to adrenaline?*

Of course you are! Everyone is. But this doesn't make anyone wrong. It's an essential component of the duality that forms your entire experience. Adrenaline is as much a part of LBC as it is of FBC. It's not *whether* you're addicted; it's *how* you feed your addiction. While other hormones undoubtedly play a role, it's abundantly clear that ecstatic states of joyous bliss are as adrenaline-fueled as the darkest scream of terror. Nightmares as well as euphoria both get their kick from the endorphins released by adrenaline.

Hopefully, you're beginning to see that living in FBC as a way of life is in some ways a smokescreen for the deeper truth of your addiction to adrenaline. Knowledge is power, and that which you do not understand can rule you with an iron fist. When you try to wrestle with fear without understanding its connection to adrenaline, failure is practically assured. The reptilian part of your brain hardwires your body to respond to adrenaline, and your addiction to this high conditions you to live in fear, which keeps the adrenaline pumping.

And around and around you go, racing madly on your very own custom chrome hamster wheel. That rush of adrenaline is what the junkie in you really seeks. The athlete hungers for it, as does the soldier and every single person choosing risky behavior of any type. And that includes you driving aggressively down the freeway.

*I'm a much safer driver than I used to be. I haven't had a ticket in decades. Well, at least not a speeding ticket.*

Whatever. We do not wish to send the message that adrenaline rushes are to be avoided; it's your unconscious addiction to them that leads to choosing risky experiences. As we have said, you avoid adrenaline only by avoiding life. Even the feeling of a deep, loving connection with another person is partially fueled by adrenaline. In this context, falling in love can be seen as the ultimate positive rush. Speaking of risky business, some say that only fools fall in love.

Loosening the control your fears have over you allows you to create more LBC in your life. And perhaps it is easier than you think to accomplish this transformation. Remember, "Fear is excitement without breath." What is the first thing you do when you become frightened? Or rather, what your body does without your conscious volition? Why, you tighten your belly and hold your breath. Right?

*Wow, now that you bring it up, I guess you're right. Whenever I contemplate my own mortality, it gives me the creeps. Just talking about it now makes me nauseous.*

So, in this moment, simply do one thing. Breathe. Breathe consciously into your belly as you become aware that you've been holding your breath, or breathing only shallowly. As you breathe, notice your posture. Are you contracted or hunched over, as though you were trying to protect your vital organs? If so, be aware that it is simply a normal part of the body's fear response. Just notice any tension, and then consciously relax. Allow your body to straighten, shoulders back, chin up. Continue breathing slowly and deeply. The fear *will* subside. It can only reign supreme when your body and breath are constricted.

As your breathing relaxes, remember that you are a Divine Soul having an earthly experience. It's natural for your body to feel fear. It's hardwired, remember? All of humanity is profoundly addicted to the adrenaline rush of fear. If you find yourself remaining in fear, dear one, simply love yourself, including your fear, and breathe. Judging yourself for feeling fear only sends you into a deepening spiral of despair. We want to emphasize that we are not referring to fear caused by imminent danger to the body, but rather non-physically threatening experiences you've been taught to fear, such as feeling as though you'll never be good enough, or perhaps even that you're unlovable.

*That's really interesting. Now that my breath has slowed, I feel much calmer. I get it. Fear is excitement without breath. I had never thought of it that way before.*

Our profound wish is that you never think of it any other way again. Now that your breathing has slowed, your body has relaxed and you have reconnected with your Divinity, you will find that you are once again able to make choices. Do you still desire adrenaline's fire? Wonderful! That's one of the multitude of gifts your body offers your consciousness. Now, however, you can *choose* the adrenaline rush of excitement rather than that of fear.

# To the Core

There is sunshine lost in shadow
Darkness dances in the light

For every nameless terror
Laughter floats free on the wind

So many lives we've lived in fear
Always running from our core

We are both, and more, but we forget
Place one in front, the other, hidden

Pretending we're not that anymore –
We disown our shadow, whatever its source

Warriors deny the peaceful way
Peacekeepers fear the warrior's tread

Each disowning their secret selves
With no clue that each needs the other to live

We're at play in duality and we ache for Home
Our highest truth, and deepest need,

Is to own to the core
That we're both sun and night –

# 26 Gratitude and Adrenaline

> Gratitude unlocks the fullness of life. It turns what we have into enough, and more. It turns denial into acceptance, chaos to order, confusion to clarity. It can turn a meal into a feast, a house into a home, a stranger into a friend. Gratitude makes sense of our past, brings peace for today, and creates a vision for tomorrow.
>
> – *Melody Beattie*

You have said many times that nothing in your life seems all that exciting anymore. We spiritedly beg to differ. Just for openers, that you are alive is truly a miracle. You have friends and family you love. Whether you are aware of it or not, they also love you dearly. We know that you have a warm, dry place to sleep, and that when you're hungry you are able to eat.

Do you feel profound gratitude for being? If not, we highly recommend that you find something or someone in your life to be grateful for. You might simply begin with gratitude for your breath. As you continue breathing slowly and deeply, allow awareness of the many gifts in your life to come forward. Be grateful for flowers, rainbows, mountain vistas, oceans, the rising and setting sun, the moon and stars, and perhaps most of all for the gentle touch of a loved one.

*You're so right! I adore nature, I really do. I just get so busy with my life that I forget to take the time to appreciate it.*

We understand. It is all too easy to forget. Just notice how, in this moment, you are present with your gratitude. Can you feel the sublime rush of this exquisite high flowing out of your heart?

*Now that you mention it, I do feel kind of funny, as though I have butterflies in my stomach. It's such an odd sensation....*

So, dear one, we ask you to breathe into that feeling. Just breathe, and notice how that feels to you.

*Um, it feels, well, good! Incredibly good, actually. It reminds me of how I felt on Christmas Eve when I was a child, or how it felt to be going to spend the night at my best friend's house. My goodness, I haven't felt like this in such a long time. Come to think of it, it's been way too long since I've seen my best friend.*

So be sure to give him a call soon. And what you're noticing is wonderful! We're delighted that you are choosing, in this moment, to allow yourself to drink in the ecstatic joy and bliss that is your birthright. Now, to emphasize the power of choice, let us revisit your fear of dying one more time.

*Bummer! You just had me feeling all gooey inside, and now you go and spoil it by bringing up death again.*

We didn't *spoil* anything. Death is part of the "isness" of life. What truly creates your experience are the stories you listen to and believe. It is what you choose to make of it. Once again, notice your breath. Did your belly constrict when I mentioned death?

*Ahhhh, yes. I can't seem to help it. It's really insidious.*

Well, it certainly is a deep neuronal pathway, though by characterizing it as insidious you give it more power, as though somehow "it" is out to get you. Simply come back to your breath, knowing that in this moment you are safe. While death is an inevitable part of life, being terrified of it is optional. As you let go of your fear, feel your entire body relax, and choose more of the infinite joy you were bathing in only a moment ago. Got it?

*Whew! I feel like a yo-yo, but I see your point. Whatever I'm paying attention to in the moment creates my experience. That's really potent!*

Potent beyond your wildest dreams, dear one. So, what changed? Your breath. Your breath and your awareness. What had been seen only as a source of fear suddenly became an opportunity. Not only is "fear excitement without breath," it is also an incredible gift. Fear is a doorway into another world, but only if you are willing to breathe into it and listen to what it has to tell you.

Everyone's higher self is always sending out messages of hope and promise, though society has unconsciously trained you to subvert these messages into waves of fear. The solution is to breathe into your fear and listen for the still, small voice inside. This voice is your higher self, the voice calling you to your highest potential. When you're ready, you will understand that this voice is none other than your personal connection to the God/Goddess you make manifest in each moment.

*You keep talking about my higher self, but I still find it difficult to believe you're serious. I have a higher self inside me?*

Dear one, of course you do, though not literally in your body. More like inside your heart. Specifically, you have *us* inside your heart. And outside as well. As we've repeatedly said, "There is no separation." Further, we teach that the heart is the nexus point out of which potentiality becomes actuality. In other words, one of the portals through which the undifferentiated love that lives at the core of manifest creation comes into being is through the heart. It is how we come to you, how everyone's higher self comes through.

And yes, absolutely *everyone* has the exquisite gift of a higher self. That's what this book is all about. The most challenging part of the soul's journey towards consciousness is often believing that it is possible in the first place. The more you accept the unconditional love of your higher self (that would be us, dear one), the more joy you will find in each moment! And so, in *this* now moment, we wish to welcome you to a more conscious life.

Now that you understand the nature of your fear, and your need for adrenaline, you have a choice. This choice is *not* about getting out of the way of the taxi. Assuming you are aware that the taxi is heading for you, your body will do its best to remove you from danger before you have time to think about it. This choice *is* about the next time you're afraid and there's no taxi in sight. As soon as you become aware of any fear, simply remember to breathe. Breathe, relax, gently straighten your body, and become present to the moment, for when you're present, you can choose love and peace. They are always available, only one choice away.

# 27 Them & Us

Friend, our closeness is this:
Anywhere you put your foot, feel me
In the firmness under you.

How is it with this love,
I see your world and not you?

– *Rumi*

*I'm beginning to understand about fear and adrenaline. Now, can we spend some time talking about karma and death? You know, before I started having these conversations with you I didn't even believe in karma, and now I'm terrified of it! Even my reservation about reincarnation is weakening, and as it does, my anxiety about what I do in this life, not to mention what I have already done, is growing stronger. I think I am actually becoming more fearful of my karma than of my death.*

*You say there's no Karmic Wheel, no Heaven or Hell, but what about sin, or true evil? Are there such things? You've said that it doesn't matter what we do, it only matters what we make of what we do. Are you saying that sin and evil don't exist? There's war, political repression, torture, child abuse, and brutality of all kinds. I get depressed just thinking about these issues. If these kinds of heinous acts aren't sinful acts of evil, then what are they?*

Actually, we did not say that it doesn't matter what you do. It matters a great deal, especially to your heart. We said that it is not the "isness" of the situation that creates your suffering, but rather how you are with the "isness." Do you understand the difference between what you do and how you are with what you do?

*Not really. I thought I had this figured out, but once again I feel confused.*

Patience, dear one. If you will recall, we've already spent a fair amount of time exploring the idea that you commonly experience the events of your lives in the context of a story. In order for a behavior to be considered sinful, or even evil, there must be some parameters, or set of values, that holds the given action in that way. Context leads you to take that action out of the realm of "isness" and into the realm of sin.

Take killing, for example. If you kill someone in defense of your family, you generally consider it justifiable homicide. If you were to kill that same person to defend your family's honor, there are some traditions that would find that normal and necessary behavior, though many of you would find it reprehensible. Then there are those who kill in cold blood, purely for profit. They have been so devalued that they find no value in life, only in ending it. Some, even more deeply wounded, torture and kill others for the thrill of the adrenaline rush. While profoundly dysfunctional, it is clear that hurting others is how they empty their emotional balloons as well as how they obtain an adrenaline fix.

To sum up: in each of these examples someone has died at another's hand. In the first, it may well be justified, in the second, not so much. None of the other deaths have any remote justification. You understand motivation only in the context of the values held by the culture within which this death occurs. The activity (killing) and the outcome (death at another's hand) are identical, it's the motivation that makes the difference in deciding whether a crime has been committed.

*So, there's no such thing as pure, unmitigated evil?*

If, by evil, you mean, "tending to cause great harm; having or exerting a malignant influence,"[25] we deeply appreciate how it can seem that way. As a species, there is no question that you have refined the art of inflicting pain and misery on each other. The history of humanity is replete with stories of tyrants and warlords who, seemingly with great joy, inflicted enormous suffering on others. You even have a word for the worst of it, at least in terms of quantity: genocide. We also agree that, by any reasonable person's standard, such acts are heinous. Sadly, they continue to this day.

The question we raise in regard to this discussion of "dirty deeds, done dirt cheap,"[26] is ***why***? Why do people treat others in such horrific ways? Many say that such people are literally possessed. We simply don't agree that "the devil made them do it." Rather, we teach that almost everyone who inflicts hurt onto another, whether by a casual backhanded slap, a cruel put-down "meant in fun," or raping and strangling a child, *learned* that behavior by having violence (in the latter case, *extreme* violence) inflicted upon them. More deeply still, we find that at the core of all wars, genocide, terrorism, domestic abuse and any other form of conflict one cares to examine, lies the story of "Them & Us."

*What do you mean by "Them & Us?"*

We're getting to that. As we said, almost everyone who violently forces their will upon another has first been violated. It doesn't matter to what degree one personally participates in this insidious, pervasive cycle, it affects everyone. Your earliest hurts feed and then reinforce your sense of separation. Most of you soon come to experience yourselves as "Us" and everyone else as "Them."

This story of "Them & Us" applies not only to your friends and family, but also to absolutely anyone who you perceive as hurting you, whether it is physical or emotional in nature. According to the simple, inexorable understanding of a child, that person *must* be separate from you, or they wouldn't be hurting you. You know you would never choose to hurt yourself, so it must be "Them" causing your pain.

You're born completely helpless, utterly trusting in others to take care of your needs. As you grow, and those you trust abuse your faith in them, you naturally become wary. For some of you, this happens almost immediately. For others, it doesn't happen until you go off to school. Eventually, almost inevitably, trust is broken. When this happens, in some sense everyone becomes a threat, everyone becomes "Them."

*Is that why I struggle so to trust others? Even my own family seems out to get me sometimes.*

As we just mentioned, for most people trust is broken at an early age. Your family sees you as one of "Them." In the context of FBC, some version of "Them and Us" plays out in virtually all families, not just yours. As you mature, you all have your share, often what seems to be way more than your share, of painful experiences. They dovetail perfectly with your growing feeling that you are separate, and that the world is not a safe place.

Over and over, your life circumstances continue to reinforce this core belief. In school, you find there are people all too happy to gossip about, tease or bully others. These children (and sometimes adults) are clearly in deep pain. They have already learned how to take their minds off their own wounds, at least momentarily, by hurting someone else.

The adult caregivers and other role models in their lives teach, by example, how to make themselves feel better at the expense of those they perceive as weaker. To avoid becoming targets of these predators, many of you join in, hoping to be seen as an ally of the attacker, thus creating a "pack" mentality that powerfully supports the Fear-Based-Consciousness story of "Them & Us" you just asked about. This same FBC, which now dominates your global society, has done so for thousands of years. Words, fists and feet eventually turn into guns, suicide bombers and germ warfare.

*So the story of "Them & Us" is what causes people to be cruel to each other?*

You've almost got it. It's not the cause; it's what enables people even to conceive of being cruel to each other. For if you truly understand that in hurting another you are actually hurting yourselves, how could you ever do it? It is only by labeling others as "Them," which is dehumanizing, that it becomes relatively easy to injure, torture and kill. It can even seem imperative to do so before "They" hurt you.

It is remarkably easy to identify "Them" by any characteristics you have been taught to perceive as being different from "Us," whether physical, cultural, behavioral, religious or otherwise. You may even invent differences that don't actually exist in order to justify treating others as "less-than." As you focus on those differences, they seem to magnify and multiply, growing ever more significant until it becomes apparent that you cannot co-exist with "Them." You must either dominate or destroy those who seem different from "Us." Of course, "They" are often having the exact same experience! The only difference between these groups is one of perspective, between who is "Us" and who is "Them."

*Oh my God! I wish I had understood this years ago. The pain I've caused....*

Everyone has, dear one. Until and unless you awaken, pain, fear and suffering are passed on from generation to generation. As twisted as this may sound, to someone deeply wounded, progeny who didn't express similar wounds would not even be recognizable as their own. At the other end of this spectrum, when you grok "Them" ***as*** "Us," it becomes almost unthinkable to do "Them" harm.

No war has ever been fought without a potent story of "Them & Us." Every political regime dominates its people by hypnotizing them with elaborate lies.[27] (Does the phrase "weapons of mass destruction" ring a bell?) Sometimes this regime identifies "Them" as living outside the boundaries of their country, or sphere of control. Quite often, though, some group within their own borders is set up as "Them."

No one has ever tortured or brutalized another human being without holding the belief that "They" somehow deserved the pain "We" were inflicting upon "Them." Similarly, only those adults caught up in some story of their own wounding routinely injure children. It is out of this pain that they feel justified or even compelled to "discipline" the child "for its own good." Unfortunately, it's easier than you might think to move from hurting outsiders objectified as "Them" to traumatizing those in your own families using the same rationalization, including babies right out of the womb.

*I am deeply saddened to realize that I have no difficulty agreeing with you. And it seems clear from what you've said that fear drives this whole process. Since Fear-Based-Consciousness is so dominant here on Earth, how can we ever hope to get past the story of "Them & Us"?*

# Drunk with Wonder

# 28 Grace is Your Birthright

Gracefulness has been defined to be the outward expression of the inward harmony of the soul.
– *William Hazlitt*

The truth is that every single person is born as an infinitely precious, perfectly divine holographic representation of God/Goddess. You were born perfect. Your parents were born perfect. Your best friend and your worst enemy were each born perfect. Mother Teresa, Adolph Hitler, Mahatma Gandhi, Osama Bin Laden, Martin Luther King, Jr., even George Bush, Dick Cheney and Donald Rumsfield; each and every person on this planet was born perfect.

Perhaps, in this moment, the health of your body seems less than perfect. Indeed, it is one of the most common laments of this or any time. From a larger perspective, however, you are still immaculately perfect just as you are. One of the clearest ways to deeply appreciate the underlying Oneness beneath your stories of "Them & Us" is to grok all the way to your toes that it is, after all, only a story, and not the "isness." Consider a newborn. What are the characteristics of an infant, aside from their dependence on others for their physical needs?

*Well, I guess innocence is the first thing that comes to mind. Innocence and curiosity. Babies are exquisitely tuned to learning. They seem to soak up knowledge like sponges. And happiness, too. Babies are naturally happy and carefree. They're also very honest; you always know if they're upset. They also seem to have an instant reset button, one minute they're happy and laughing, the next thing you know they're screaming, then they're right back to being happy. Their resilience always astonishes me.*

Babies require no training in the honest expression of their feelings, they are pure bundles of innocence. Their brains haven't wired themselves up yet in response to their environment and experiences. When they are feeling loved, they laugh and coo and generally act in totally adorable ways. When they're hungry or frightened, they cry, even scream, for attention. When their needs are met, they immediately return to a state of happiness. All too often, training that particular characteristic out of them is one of the first things parents do.

Even in this so-called enlightened age, with numerous studies to the contrary, many parents still let their babies cry themselves to sleep. This is supposed to teach them not to be so dependent. The truth is, babies are inherently dependent on others. Leaving them alone to cry in their crib only teaches them that the world isn't a safe place, that their needs aren't important. Eventually, they make what feels like being abandoned mean that they aren't valued as people.

Ultimately, when you aren't valued, it becomes easy to turn around and devalue others, and away you go into "Them & Us."

*I must admit that your explanation makes a lot more sense than anything else I've heard. I guess I always thought that's just what life does to us.*

In fact, the things that happen *to* you have less to do with the kind of person you become than your interpretation of those things. In other words, it's what *you* choose to make them mean.

*Wait a minute. I've always believed that people are products of their experiences. My logic has always led me to a conclusive understanding that there is only one best choice under any given set of circumstances. If I'm thinking clearly, and acting in accordance with my understanding, then there can be only one logical response. Are you saying that's not true?*

What we are saying is that your possible responses to any given situation are bracketed by the stories within which you live. The fact is, you never really have any *direct* experiences. The way your brain works, every event that happens in your life is automatically processed through the filters of your stories, which as we've seen are comprised of previously stored events. It is this interpretation, rather than the "isness," that you perceive. It is in this way that meaning for all events is created. This is such a critical point we want to take a moment to make sure this is making sense to you.

*Actually, I'm feeling kind of lost. I don't buy for one minute that my reading the words in this book is "subject to interpretation," as you put it. They're words, for heaven's sake! English words. That's all they are. They have specifically attributed meanings, which we can look up in the dictionary. If we didn't agree on the meanings of words, we couldn't even be having this dialogue.*

That's true enough, as far as it goes. What we are working towards here is for you to get past your automatic stories about your experiences, including what you make words mean. We want you to understand *how* meaning, or context, becomes associated with "isness."

Let's use an example that is right at hand. At this moment, as you read these words, what is really going on? The "isness" goes something like this: presumably, you're holding an object composed of many pieces of paper glued together. There are squiggles, lines, and dots arranged in horizontal rows, with spaces here and there. Photons of light are reflecting from the surface of the paper as well as the ink, carrying information to light-sensitive receptors, called rods and cones, in your retinas. The receptors convert these photons into electro-chemical signals, which after some preliminary processing travel along your optic nerves to the visual cortex of your brain. There, the information is compared with a library of images, compiled from a lifetime of experiences, and is then determined to represent words in a language called English.

Once the nature of the image is established, it is transferred to another part of your brain, where further processing determines which words they are, how they relate to each other and, eventually, their probable meaning. This highly processed data package is then considered in the context of all other information in your short and long-term memories to establish how the new information relates to all other information you have previously assimilated. If acceptance of the new information requires a significant reassessment of your belief system, especially values you have labeled as yours, you will probably have feelings of resistance.

Take a moment now to check in with your breath. Is it flowing soft and easy, or does your chest feel constricted? Your breath does not lie. Remember, you're safe here. Whatever you make these words mean lies within the framework of your life. You may feel bored, angry, excited, reflective or confused. The photons are the same, they hit the receptors in your eyes the same; it's the context your stories provide that gives them a particular meaning. You can see that, whatever your reaction, it has only a little to do with the reflection of photons off the printed page.

The same is true of every experience you've ever had in your life. You've never *directly* experienced anything. Your perception of any given situation has *always* been your interpretation of it filtered first through one or more of your senses, and then always through the beliefs you hold about yourself and the world around you, which we call your stories. Does it make more sense now?

*Yes, although I must admit that I'm still having strong feelings of resistance, as you put it. I guess what I'm really struggling with is the idea that who I am is virtually independent of what has ever happened to me. In some ways, that's a deeply disconcerting idea.*

It is disconcerting because it is empowering. As long as you tell yourself the story that you are a victim of your circumstances, you don't have to accept any accountability for the life that you create. Of course, if that story is true, then you are essentially a helpless victim. If, however, you accept our contention that you have the ability to choose how you will interpret every experience in your life, including whatever meaning you give any particular event, then you are powerful indeed! You become the author of your life, capable of deliberately choosing the beliefs you will hold, the values you will use to filter your experiences, and, ultimately, the way in which you will respond to each of life's challenges and opportunities.

## Grace

There is Grace
In the moment
Or not at all

There is no time
To be here
Free of the dream

Framing the past
And the future –
We seek salvation

At the hands
Of another
In another place

At another time
But the Kingdom
Is only here and now

Through the Grace
Of infinities
Gentle heart

We are born
Forever new
In the stillness –

# 29 The Miracle of Choice

> We who lived in concentration camps can remember the men who walked through the huts comforting others, giving away their last piece of bread. They may have been few in number, but they offer sufficient proof that everything can be taken from a man but one thing: the last of the human freedoms – to choose one's attitude in any given set of circumstances, to choose one's own way.
>
> – *Viktor Frankl*

*I can see how this idea of having choices would work in most of my mundane, day-to-day experiences, but what about the really big, life-defining events?*

It is *especially* so with these. Please don't misunderstand, we are not suggesting such events are not real, or that horrible, painful things don't happen. Certainly, life can be filled with trials and tribulations, and these sometimes *appear* to shape your destiny, but that is where the illusion comes in. Ultimately, you do choose how you will interpret *every* experience in your life.

Perhaps an example will illustrate what we mean. Throughout human history there have been many stories illustrating the human potential to rise above the most trying of circumstances. Even in the midst of extraordinary pain and hardship, some people find a way to become kinder and more compassionate.

This story is about a man named Vicktor Frankl, a Jewish psychiatrist in Vienna, Austria. In 1942, Viktor was arrested by the Nazis, and along with his father, his mother, his brother and his new wife, was sent to a concentration camp. They were separated, stripped of all possessions and transferred to various facilities. For three years, Viktor endured unspeakable cruelty at the hands of his Nazi torturers. His wife, his parents and his brother perished.

In the face of these tragedies, Viktor still found reason to live. He began observing those attitudes and beliefs that enabled some to survive in the midst of wanton horror. He also studied the guards, making a conscious choice to have compassion for them. Victor felt the anguish gnawing at their core and remained compassionate, even as the guards expressed their inner agony by torturing and slaughtering an entire culture.

Compassion for an oppressor is a clear indication that the individual choosing this path recognizes the underlying unity between "Them & Us." You only need think of Jesus, Buddha, Ghandi, Martin Luther King, Nelson Mandela, Mother Teresa, the Dalai Lama, Thich Nhat Hanh and so many others to realize the profound truth revealed here.

Ultimately, Viktor came to see a deep purpose for his life. If he could survive, he would teach others that compassion is possible regardless of the ordeal being endured. In later years, Viktor wrote his story in his profoundly inspiring book, *Man's Search for Meaning*, inspiring millions of people to examine their own beliefs and values.

# 30 Choosing Beliefs and Values

> Underlying all the Dalai Lama's methods there is a set of basic beliefs that act as a substrate for all his actions: a belief in the fundamental gentleness and goodness of all human beings, a belief in the value of compassion, a belief in a policy of kindness, and a sense of commonality among all living creatures.
> – *Howard C. Cutler*

*That's an inspiring story, but I still don't understand how to go about choosing my beliefs and values, let alone changing them. I mean, aren't these pretty much set by the time we become adults?*

There are certain basic characteristics of your personality that will always be present, but this change is not only possible, it is inevitable. The crucial factor in change is not *whether* it will happen, it is *who* or *what* is directing it. Is the impetus for what is changing coming from the outside or the inside?

It may be helpful to understand more about how your beliefs and values are formed. Let's imagine for a moment that you are two years old. You are out playing in the front yard on a warm spring day, a gentle breeze ruffling your hair. The grass is new green, bright yellow dandelions dancing in the sun, the azure sky framed with fluffy white clouds. You are lost in wonder, without a care in the world. You're filled with the magic of the sights, smells, sounds, tastes and textures surrounding you.

Suddenly an outrageously colorful butterfly floats into view! Enchanted, you reach for it and it flutters away. Laughing, carefree, you run after this fantastic creature with your arms extended. Out of nowhere, a giant grabs you around the waist in one mighty hand, then holds you in the air and smacks you on the butt with the other as she screams, "Don't run out in the street! You'll get hit by a car!"

You are two years old. You know little of streets and cars. The message, while well intentioned, is meaningless to you at that level, though Mom's communication did have several lasting physiological and emotional effects. One of these effects was the creation of a belief that it is not OK for you to be that happy and carefree, that if you're having too much fun something bad is sure to occur.

Here's what happened: when your mother screamed in your ear as she snatched you up and whacked your butt, a cascade of hormones drenched your body. Adrenaline flooded into your cells, tying the memory of feeling carefree together with the intense rush of panic emanating from your Mom. From that time forward, you began imposing limits on your own happiness by subtly sabotaging your own joy. These limits will continue to color your life until you become aware of them and consciously begin to make different choices.

As you get older, a fundamental reason you maintain such beliefs is that they reinforce your sense of being helpless victims of your experience. Your identification with being a victim becomes so strong that you mistake your wounds for who you really are. "I'm wounded, therefore I am," has become a common, even foundational, belief.

It's *absolutely crucial* to understand that once this belief is formed, you hold on to it at a cellular level. Consciously, you would never choose to let this belief run your life. The subconscious, however, takes everything quite literally. The more negative the input it receives, the more it supports this type of outcome. One of the basic laws of human awareness is that, "What we hold in our consciousness we make manifest."

When you constantly affirm your belief that you can never be happy, your subconscious powerfully aligns with that story. Therefore, even though you don't recognize the existence of the belief at a conscious level, your subconscious is always looking for ways to reaffirm its validity. So, as happiness threatens to enter your life, you inevitably end up sabotaging it. Your subconscious says something to the effect of, "We're wounded, remember? We can't ever be happy. It's just not possible for us!" Your limiting belief becomes self-fulfilling.

*Wow, what a vicious cycle. How can anyone ever break out of it?*

By awakening to the subconscious! Awareness of the power of the subconscious, and how it can either support or sabotage your desires, puts your experiences into perspective. The subconscious, in concert with the conscious mind, are powerful tools for manifesting that which you desire.

An important discernment is required here. Many times you react to situations with less than full awareness (to say the least), and these reactions are born in the subconscious. When you remain unaware of these stories, the subconscious can greatly influence your evaluation of a situation in ways you would never consciously choose. As you have just seen, this is a powerful manifesting force. For you to be able to consciously harness this power, it is critical that you recognize its source.

When you begin to recognize how your subconscious makes choices for you without filtering it through the conscious mind, you have already begun the remedy. Your awareness of this process is proof that consciousness has reaffirmed its presence. The conscious mind, aided and abetted by the subconscious, can make choices for your highest good in a dynamic, fully aware environment. Once you make this realization and begin using this innate quality of your being, your life will shift dramatically towards your desired outcomes.

# 31 Emotional Icebergs and your Personal Titanic

We must be the change we wish to see in the world.

– *Mahatma Gandhi*

*That's amazing! I don't know if I can accept all of this, but if it's true, it sounds as though I can really control the direction of my life.*

We assure you that it's not only possible, but that many thousands of people have already made great strides in becoming conscious co-creators of their lives. As just one example, a non-profit organization known as Challenge Day[28] demonstrates this principle every day. They touch the hearts of tens of thousands of youth every year, going into hundreds of middle and high schools to deliver full-day programs teaching about healthy emotional expression, celebrating diversity and awakening to the passion within. Challenge Day teaches that behaviors such as bullying, teasing and violence are learned behaviors. They are examples of ways some people have been taught to empty their emotional balloons.

We want to share with you an analogy they use that is quite appropriate in illustrating the principles at work here. Imagine an iceberg, floating in the Arctic Ocean. When you look at this iceberg from the perspective of a boat resting on the water's surface, what percentage of its total mass do you think you actually see?

*Oh, I've heard about this. Probably no more than around 10%.*

That's right. In most cases, about 90% of an iceberg's mass lies hidden below the waterline. Now, think about the iceberg as an analogue of a person's personality. Most humans go through life showing perhaps 10% of who they really are, if that. Just as the iceberg keeps most of itself submerged, you use social masks you think others will find acceptable to shield your tender, vulnerable inner selves. The parts of your personalities that you were taught are not acceptable, including your unfelt feelings and your innermost instinctual needs and desires, remain deeply hidden in the subconscious.

You see, most of you don't dare to acknowledge the immense truth of who you really are. You are terrified that anyone, including yourself, would ever see your most deeply buried doubts, insecurities, unanswered questions, dreams, passions, desires and fantasies. Ironically, this realm is the seat of your authentic power!

You are petrified of becoming more visible lest you be rejected. Why? Because you've been taught that most of these disowned qualities are unattractive and signs of weakness, so you hide them from others as well as yourself. You have become experts at pretending they aren't real. You simply act as if they don't exist. In psychological terms, this is known as denial. This is so vital for you to understand that I would appreciate it if you would reread this last part.

*OK, I read it again, but I think I'm still missing something. So what if we all have shadows that we don't talk about. What's the big deal?*

The big deal is that your shadow, which includes the unacknowledged and disowned parts of you, runs your life! Just as with the iceberg analogy, when the conscious 10% finds itself in conflict with the subconscious 90%, the subconscious wins out nearly every time. Since the subconscious is where you keep most of your stories, *it* is what effectively runs you. Whenever you find yourself saying or doing something that doesn't serve you or the people in your life (and you wonder, "Where did that come from?"), we guarantee that it came from this place deep inside.

The vastness of who you *really* are remains hidden from you, because you learned early on, at a subconscious level, systematically to deny its very existence. Is it any wonder that you find it so challenging to break free of self-sabotaging patterns and achieve the outcomes you repeatedly insist you desire in life?

In order to be whole beings, living out of the authentic power of your full potential, you must be able to know and accept *all* of who you are. You need to mount an expedition into the undiscovered country of your subconscious in order to uncover what's been lurking below the waterline. It is then crucial to lovingly bring your disowned parts into the light of day, and not merely accept but come to treasure the unique spark of God that you are.

# Drunk with Wonder

# Buried

I did not know
I could get that low

Buried beneath my excavations
Into the heart of my sorrow

I lay trapped for eons,
Mountains of rotting stories

Carrying me deeper
Into the heart of darkness –

Writhing in terminal agony
I scream my name in vain

Only to choke on my stories
Of lack and exquisite shame

Like some demented drunk
Drowning in his own piss

While an angel of mercy
Tenderly holds his cold hands

And waits with gossamer grace
For another story to emerge,

Phoenix-like, from the
Abandoned ruins

Of his
Infinite imagination –

# 32 Treasuring Ourselves

> The first love affair we need to consummate is with ourselves, because only then will we be ready for relationships with others.
> – *Nathaniel Brandon*

*I suppose that some people may need to go through this process of self-discovery and acceptance, but not me! I already accept myself just the way I am. I can, however, readily think of several people who would benefit from such an expedition.*

Can you not accept them just as they are? The truth is, everyone craves acceptance from others as well as themselves. It's one of your most basic needs. The reason for this is obvious, once you think about it. Humans evolved as pack animals. Acceptance as part of the pack conferred huge survival advantages on your ancestors, just as it does now. As much as you may like to think of yourselves as independent and self-reliant, very few humans alive would survive more than a handful of days stripped of the protections and conveniences of modern society.

*Whatever. It's still not my problem if other people don't accept me.*

No? Can you truly not see your own denial here? The need for acceptance, rather than being a character flaw that ought to be denied in favor of a story of the rugged individualist, is as fundamental to your being as your need for food. In your fast-paced world, these compulsive and often contradictory needs to be right and to be accepted, coupled with your instinct to avoid discomfort, routinely result in a form of paralysis. They lock you into an irrational immobility restricting your adaptability to your ever-changing environment. Once you embrace your profound need for acceptance by family and friends – your tribe, if you will – you can begin to reassess, and perhaps shift, some of your most basic personal stories. This intense longing can be traced back to the primal emotion labeled "separation anxiety."

*This makes a lot of sense, but it doesn't explain people who always have to be right about everything. I find them most annoying. Of course I'm not like that. I really pride myself on staying open-minded.*

We can see that, and we commend you. Please be aware that these characteristics, including the need for acceptance, being right and avoiding discomfort, are all basic to human nature. It is when they become habitual that you can get into trouble. When you decide you are right about something without thinking it through, it is easy to miss even better solutions. For example, when you avoid the often very real discomfort of exercise, your body deteriorates and you die much earlier than you otherwise might.

Needing to be right as well as accepted is at the core of your social relationships. You mentioned how annoying you find others who always have to be right. Perhaps you've come across the question, "Which would you prefer, to be right or to have friends?"

*You mean I have to choose? But sometimes I am right, damnit!*

You may very well be, but so what? Does that make you a better person? Does being right still feel good if it costs you friendships? When you need to make sure others acknowledge your being right, you leave no room for them to have an opinion, and no room for compromise. It is one thing to be right if that taxi is about to hit you, and another thing entirely to argue over which is the better team. A sure sign of Awakening is when you are authentically connected with your own truth, yet feel no need to foist that truth onto others.

We appreciate that it can seem to be of the highest importance to feel justified in the beliefs concerning yourself and the world around you. Any doubt about those justifications will likely manifest as uneasiness. Whenever people step out of their comfort zone, particularly in regard to examining their foundational stories, some level of apprehension is sure to manifest. It is then an easy step to rationalize these moments of conflict so they fall into alignment with their stories and beliefs, re-establishing a state of seeming harmony.

We will show you what we mean. Let's consider your response to our statement that all humans have a need to be right. Actually, the annoying people you referred to ("Them") are simply those who have become so proficient at denial that they are totally unaware of how obvious their need to always be right is to others ("Us"). Imagine walking around with your zipper down, or a piece of broccoli stuck in your teeth, blissfully ignorant of something others see quite clearly. When you need to be right in order to feel comfortable in your own skin, your denial of this need keeps you from seeing what seems obvious to others.

*Well, I certainly hope that if someone were to share this kind of information with me, I would accept it gracefully, even if it was only to avoid any further embarrassment.*

Hmmm, it might be interesting to note that you didn't experience any embarrassment at all until you discovered, or were told, that your zipper was open. In any event, what would be so wrong in pulling your zipper up with a flourish in front of a thousand people who have come to hear you speak?

*I'm speaking to a thousand people and my zipper's down? Oh my God! I've never even considered a possibility like that. I pray nothing that embarrassing ever happens to me.*

This story is simply another opportunity to see that it's not who witnesses the zipping, it's what you make of it. Instead of choosing acute embarrassment, you could say, as you zip, "Show's over!" Or perhaps, "Now that I have your attention…." Making light of the situation humanizes you to your audience, instantly defusing any embarrassment. Some people actually do such things on purpose, in order to gain an audience's attention. This tactic is known as a pattern interrupt, and is a (hopefully more successful) version of the Wizard of Oz's frantic yet futile admonition to, "Pay no attention to the man behind the curtain!"

*I learned early on that things such as zipper interruptus were shameful under any circumstances, perhaps even a sign of senility. It makes me shudder just thinking about being seen that way in public.*

We understand how you might feel that way. It is important, though, to realize that your reaction is a *learned* response, not at all innate or instinctual. It's really just a habit.

# 33 The Pearl of Personality

The more you praise and celebrate your life,
the more there is in life to celebrate.
– *Oprah Winfrey*

Let us show you what we mean. Take your hands and lace your fingers together in front of you. Now, which thumb is on top?

*My right thumb. So what?*

Just bear with us a moment. Now, re-lace your fingers so your left thumb is on top. How does that feel?

*Really quite weird, in kind of an uncomfortable way.*

Do you know what all of this means about you?

*Well, probably that I'm right-handed, or maybe that I'm right-brained?*

Actually, though your answers are most plausible, it doesn't mean anything. It is simply an example of a habit. You began lacing your fingers together that way in your mother's womb. Others have their left thumb on top, and some people's thumbs rest side by side. These "natural" positions for interlaced fingers has nothing to do with a person being right or left-handed. It is simply an example of how doing something repeatedly creates neuronal pathways, and over time it becomes increasingly easy to confuse these pathways, or habits, with being right. Adding an addictive drug such as adrenaline confuses the issue even more.

The point is that whenever you feel uneasy, performing a habitual ritual can feel soothing. It's called being in your comfort zone. As we've said, the subconscious, which contains these neuronal pathways, is where your comfort zone and habitual patterns are sustained. For many of you, needing to be right is a deep neuronal pathway,[29] so much so that simply allowing for the *possibility* of not knowing can feel extremely uncomfortable.

*You got that right! I'm feeling way uncomfortable just talking about it.*

That's wonderful news! It means that we are on the right track. As uncomfortable as it may feel, being out of your comfort zone is the only place you can grow. One of the reasons for your discomfort is that you use habits, including substance abuse, to self-medicate. When you are emotionally wounded, physically abused or otherwise exposed to events that cause trauma, you instinctively seek ways to alleviate your pain. It is really a survival technique. When this happens, you often come to strongly identify with your wounds. As we have said, this identification can become so potent that your story contains some version of, "I'm wounded, therefore I am." Despite your best efforts, that part of you which identifies with these wounds actively resists all attempts to heal them.

*But, that's crazy. Why would we do that? More specifically, why would I do that? It sounds so counter-productive.*

When you are wounded, especially early on, your trauma forms a significant part of the nucleus of your personality. To that part of you, healing those hurts feels like death itself. Your life experiences, including your wounds, are like the grain of sand in the oyster around which the pearl forms. From your perspective, trying to heal your wounds so that they no longer exist, even as memories, is like drilling into the pearl to root out the grain of sand. While the grain of sand may indeed be removed, the pearl is destroyed in the process.[30]

To put this idea into another perspective, some teachings hold that what we're calling the "pearl of personality" is none other than the illusory self stigmatized as the ego. By "illusory Self," we simply mean the part of God-As-Us that identifies with separation. In these traditions, the ego is seen as the cause of attachment and suffering, and much energy is spent in an effort to root out this illusory miscreant. Enlightenment is seen as the transcendence of the ego, and ego death as crucial to this process.

*Ouch! That doesn't sound like much fun to me.*

It isn't. From our perspective, the whole process actually continues the dance of contentious duality, in the form of the ego and that which transcends, or wins out only after a long, fierce struggle. It is our contention that this is no more useful to most of you than drilling out the grain of sand would be to enhance a pearl.

Our goal is to show you how to cradle these wounds so that this part of you feels safe and loved just the way it is, and then to actually embrace and own them as part of what makes you the unique and glorious gift you are. We want to help you celebrate every part of you, including all the parts that have remained hidden under the waterline. Every single experience you've ever had is a gift, even though it isn't gift-wrapped. In the next chapter, we are going to show you how the hardest times in your life also contain the greatest blessings.

# 34 Healing Your Core Wounds: Dropping the Waterline

The true task of spiritual life is not found in faraway places or unusual states of consciousness. It is here in the present. It asks of us a welcoming spirit to greet all that life presents to us with a wise, respectful, and kindly heart. We can bow to both beauty and suffering, to our entanglements and confusion, to our fears and to the injustices of the world. Honoring the truth in this way is the path to freedom.

– *Jack Kornfield*

*I have no clue how the worst times of my life could have any gifts, let alone great ones. I must admit, though, that it is becoming much clearer how my stories form my experience of the world. They really are the fabric of my life. I can even see how re-examining some of my stories could be very useful for expanding my awareness, but what if I have some that I'm afraid to look at?*

Actually, that is the critical issue here. When you own the truth of your most deeply hidden stories, you are dropping the waterline around the iceberg of your subconscious, exposing the frigid wasteland of your fears to the warmth of light and love. It is when these stories remain hidden under the waterline that they run you. And while there is value in examining even the smallest issue, it is crucial for you to understand that the stories you least want to examine are the very ones most likely to contain the keys to your freedom.

In fact, you will probably find that some of the stories you are avoiding are actually linked to deeper, more painful ones which you long ago banished to your subconscious. These are your core wounds. As you dig down to the layer of stories just above them, it is quite common to become extremely defensive. Like many untended lesions, your core wounds continue to fester. Though your victim stories form scabs, the pain continues throbbing in the background. You must be willing to gently open and cleanse these wounds so that they may heal.

*Wow, I'm noticing a familiar nervousness. I think this is the point where I normally distract myself. I recognize that I'm feeling fearful, although I'm not sure of what. I'm noticing the metallic taste of adrenaline, my palms are sweaty, and I'm struggling to take a deep breath. Even so, I'm determined to explore this realm. Please, tell me again where our core wounds come from?*

First, we congratulate you on noticing your breath! You are truly making fabulous progress. Your courage in the face of your fear is most inspiring!

As to where your core wounds come from, most of them happen at a very early age. Quite similar to the earlier story of the two-year-old punished for chasing the butterfly into the street, the actual event might have seemed insignificant. It's what you make it mean that is huge. In every case with these deep core wounds, there is a point in the process below the conscious level where it becomes a foundational story. The foundational stories of entire cultures are built in much the same fashion.

Remember, these stories became locked in cellular memory by the flood of primal emotions triggered by your perception of the event. Future triggers into this wound could be as seemingly mundane as a tone of voice, a look, a smell, or anything associated with that experience. The trigger starts a chain reaction in the amygdala that recreates the flood of hormones and the concomitant overwhelming trauma of the original wound.

For instance, in the example of the two-year-old, there was an expectation of continuing to run and play with the butterfly. When reality suddenly changed, the story had to change along with it, in order to reconcile it with the "isness" of the experience. *How* the story changed in that moment is where the "choice point" lives, where you give the experience the specific meaning that wounds your young heart so deeply.

*You keep saying that I choose to make the "isness" mean something, but could I really, at the age of two, made that kind of choice? Wouldn't it have simply been more of an emotional response?*

From your current perspective as an adult, it certainly might seem so, though there is nothing simple or unimportant about emotional responses. It is crucial to grok that it is *specifically* these responses, *not* your thinking, that adrenaline locks into your cellular memory. Long before the age of two, much earlier than your understanding of the logic you later associate with them, you are making choices.

In truth, you make *all* choices using some form of discernment. For the most part, the rational process you apparently go through as you make them is no more than window dressing, an illusion constructed to justify the choice you truly desire. Many times you become so enamored with this illusion that you override discernment and make choices that you know in your heart are not for your highest good, simply because they appear more able to scratch the itch of short-term gratification.

*But can a child really make discerning choices?*

Absolutely. While it is true that the ability to logically think through choices is not available to young children, choices are constantly being made, whether or not the information or understanding of the consequences is sufficient. As parents, you may feel intensely that your children are making mistakes that should be corrected, but the only way children actually learn is by having the opportunity to experience the consequences of their choices as often as possible.

When you as children make choices that don't work for you, and have the opportunity to experience unwelcome consequences, it becomes possible to learn something. When well-meaning adults shield you from life's lessons, it becomes much more challenging to understand that you are responsible for the quality of your life. You can only learn independent, critical thinking through practice. Whichever you practice, making choices or being a victim, you will incorporate the relevant lessons into your most basic stories. You then defend these stories as the very core of who you are, both consciously and, most importantly, subconsciously.

To illustrate, let us look again at our example of the butterfly and the two-year-old. As she grew up, some of her thoughts about that experience might have included, "It's not OK for me to be this happy. How stupid of me, I should have known better. I'm clumsy and accident prone, so I need to be rescued from danger." You've no doubt encountered people who routinely make similar kinds of self-sabotaging choices.

*Can I tell you a story about something that happened to a friend of mine when he was four years old?*

Yes, of course, please do.

*It seems that his immediate family was visiting with relatives in another state. He remembers attempting to stay close to his mother, because he didn't feel secure in these unfamiliar surroundings. Then, someone suggested going somewhere. All he remembers is that everyone left the house and wound up standing on the curb near some cars. The rest of the family climbed in while he waited for his mother to tell him which vehicle to climb into.*

*To his absolute horror, no one said anything to him before the doors closed and the cars drove off. He was left standing there, utterly alone. His mother later told him that they got no further than a block away before she asked where he was and recognized he'd been left behind. They came back immediately, though it seemed an eternity to him. In his mother's defense he felt compelled to add that she had two other children to attend to. His four-year-old self, however, surprisingly overlooked this fact.*

That must have been traumatic for him. Do you know how this affected his life?

*Yes! He told me that he remembers wondering, as he stood there, why he hadn't been included. He thought that they must not want him with them. It wasn't until many years later that he realized he had trouble joining unfamiliar groups, and many years later still before he finally associated this incident with that particular personality trait.*

Thank you for sharing your friend's story. This is a perfect example of a core wound. He made a decision about who he was based on an intense emotional experience. His parents did not intend to leave him; he was simply overlooked in the chaos of the moment. His small self made it mean that he was worth less. What got triggered in him was separation anxiety, one of those primal emotions we've been talking about.

From where he now sits, it's clear that there were other choices available, though as a four-year-old it would have been most unusual for him to have made any of them. Other choices might have included not attaching any emotional significance to the event, or believing that he was tough and he could handle it. At the other end of the spectrum, he could have chosen something such as, "I am dearly loved, and that's why my Mom came back for me." Since this happened early in his life, it formed a core part of his identity, one he may still be working through.

*I've often wondered why he chose such a negative connotation? I know it was traumatic, but they did come right back for him. Didn't that show him that they loved and wanted him?*

Of course it did, but his separation anxiety was already triggered. Also, we have no doubt he must have been primed for this story by other events in his life. You said he was four when this happened. Do you know if a younger sibling had come into his family?

*Yes, actually. How did you know?*

Based on his story, it seemed likely that he had already been through something that deeply affected him. When younger siblings come onto the scene, people often make it mean that they aren't wanted, or at least aren't enough by themselves. You can imagine how, from a primal perspective, a sibling might represent a rival for scarce resources, including loving attention from parents.

In your case, for example, your mother left you to have another baby. That's almost impossible for a young child to understand. They just feel as though they've been supplanted, replaced or even abandoned. Your friend may have thought, "There they go again," when they left him on the sidewalk. It reinforced a story he was already telling himself.

# A Small Boy

Traveling back in time to an earlier day,
I saw myself as a small boy laughing, at play

And I was struck by the way my tiny body moved,
As though it hadn't yet been caught in the groove

Of overwhelming guilt and fear, the innocence
Of youth intact, no need for strong defense –

I gazed into those clear blue eyes
And saw mirrored there a cloudless sky,

With my light blond locks and bright teeth flashing
I suppose you could say I looked almost dashing

In my little boy pants and my wide-open stance
As I sang to the tune of my own inner dance –

I wanted to run up and hug that small boy,
Wrap him in love and cloak him with joy,

He didn't know, he hadn't yet learned
What it's like to get badly burned

By the gnawing pain of growing up –
But now I'm a grown up

And my heart has all but closed –
If I could just hose

Off my emotions, set them in a tub of love to soak,
Then I could travel back once more, remove my cloak

Of sorrow and pick that little boy up in my arms,
Give him the courage to meet any harm,

Hold him close to my beating heart,
Make living together our highest art,

For you see, he is my oldest friend,
Someday, together, we will ascend –

# 35 Letting go of Victim Consciousness

I believe there are more urgent and honorable occupations than the incomparable waste of time we call suffering.

– *Colette*

*Oh, I see. His story of being left behind on the sidewalk has actually been covering a deeper one that came from his baby sister being born. I'm still not sure, though, why he made those events so traumatic. He still thinks it means that he's weak or something.*

Not at all. It's a result of evolution. In the unforgiving world of your ancestors, it was of the highest priority to take all threats seriously. If any one of your ancestors failed to learn from just one serious mistake, or had just one case of ill-timed overconfidence, you wouldn't be here contemplating these issues. When triggered by an event you perceive as threatening, your brain is hardwired to bypass thinking and switch on the fight or flight mechanism. This wiring is located in the amygdala, on top of the brain stem, the seat of your most basic autonomic functions. Perhaps you remember us speaking of this earlier?

This fight-or-flight instinct immediately kicks up the production of adrenaline, dilating some blood vessels while constricting others so that blood can rapidly be concentrated in those parts of the body where it may be needed most. You are no doubt aware that such a mechanism exists, but you might be surprised to learn that this "on" switch appears to have no corresponding "off" switch for when the threat has passed. It is only as the body metabolizes the adrenaline that it is able to relax.

*I have noticed that it takes me a long time to calm down after I feel an adrenaline rush, even when I consciously attempt to do so.*

This is exactly what we're talking about. Another point we want to emphasize is that these primal emotions are often triggered by perceived threats that are not physical in nature. Going back to your friend's story, he experienced a profound fear-based adrenaline rush caused by his sense of abandonment. This activated both panic and separation anxiety, deepening his core story of not being enough.

From an evolutionary perspective, being part of a clan or tribe afforded a major survival advantage, so your ancestors were very careful to avoid being kicked out of the "family." This is the root of most acceptance issues, thereby forming the basis for many of the fascinating strategies you employ so others will accept you. Again, if any of your ancestors had failed this test, they wouldn't be your ancestors and you wouldn't be here now.

These are just a few examples of how you are hard-wired through evolution to place great emphasis on perceived threats. Even today, in the midst of your high-tech civilization, these primal instincts are still very much with you. fMRI brain scans conclusively show that you have major neuronal pathways from your senses straight into your amygdala, but no corresponding pathways back out.

That's why, when you get triggered into one of your core stories of fear and lack, it can feel like such a monumental effort to ascend from the pit of darkness and return to love. Your sense of self gets stuck, and it can feel as though you're never going to find your way out. Have you ever experienced getting in an argument with someone, then realizing it's petty and plain not worth it, only to discover that you just can't seem to get off it? You must become aware that these primal drives are still active in your life, and that this pit of darkness is a real neuronal trap, before you can learn how to stop them from running you.

*I know that one! I just hadn't heard that there was a scientifically based reason for that helpless feeling of being stuck in FBC. No wonder most of us have a tendency to place greater emphasis on core survival issues than on developing a positive self-image. Now that I'm aware of this, is my life going to become easier?*

Quite possibly, especially if by "easier" you mean less suffering. As we have seen, you manifest suffering for yourself when you make any given situation, or "isness," mean something that creates Fear-Based-Consciousness. The point is, you make every core wound you experience mean whatever best fits the story you are living in that moment. Those key elements of your story continue to have a profound impact on you until you are able to resolve them. Once you feel complete with your past you can begin choosing new, life-affirmimng stories. These stories can make the "isness" of your past into an ally for your awakening.

Virtually all people are wounded, traumatized by various events in their lives. And, since your need to perpetuate your stories is so strong, you actually nurture your core wounds by regularly sabotaging yourselves so that your story continues to make itself, and you, "right". The payoff is that you proceed pretty much as you have all your lives, with your core wounds at the center of your experience, as in, "I'm wounded, therefore I am."

You vigorously fight to retain your wounds, allowing you to sustain your helpless victim story. Of course, as you have so eloquently put it, what you are really doing is staying stuck in FBC. Breaking this pattern, this deep neuronal pathway, is essential to awakening in time and becoming fully present in the moment. And, as we've seen, it is only when you are present that choice is available. Thus, exploring your core wounds is a critical step in creating a positive direction in your life.

*Wow! You really nailed it! I feel as though I'm finally getting a sense of what you're talking about, and I'm ready to make a declaration.*

Awesome! Please continue.

***I hereby choose to let go of my victim consciousness!*** *I'm determined to change what I make my stories mean, though I'm still feeling some confusion as to exactly how to go about it.*

Bravo! That is a potent declaration, and we will do everything we can to support you. As for how to go about it, it's as simple as noticing your stories in the moment, choosing what you want to make them mean, and then acting on your new choices.

For example, let us imagine a friend who finds herself to be a repeated target of humiliation at work. These attacks make your friend angry and resentful, generally ruining her day. When your friend remembers to breathe and become present to the "isness," she realizes that this aggressor is emotionally wounded, and that these attacks aren't even about her. Instead of choosing to believe the attacker's vitriol and sink into the pit we've been talking about, she chooses not to give her power away. This way she's able to stay above the fray.

# 36 All God, All the Time

> There's nowhere we can go, and nothing we can do, that will bring us any closer to God than we are right here and right now.
>
> – *Anonymous*

You see, when you are wounded very early in life, and then come to identify with that wound, you are exquisitely set up to spend the rest of your life wrapped in the drama, operating out of Fear-Based-Consciousness. This is no mistake. Remember, God-As-Us loves drama, and the purpose of your existence is to fully experience the drama of your life as God in human form. Don't forget that it's *all* God, *all* the time.

Your need to identify with and defend your core wounds can be seen as a profoundly compelling way to set up the game here on Earth, at least the way it has been played so far. Fear-Based-Consciousness is intoxicating! An infinite number of amazing adventures await the hero who must save the damsel in distress, or save "your people" from the Infidels or the Christian hordes. Perhaps you have heard it said that, "My God is better than your God."

Though you had limited choices as a child, you now have many more. If you choose to continue playing the game from the fear-based, defensive perspective of your wounded child, you will keep on producing high drama. Please note that this melodrama is still God-As-Us, acting out the Great Passion Play. It's *not* wrong. However, if you're tired of suffering, or perhaps even bored with it, you can jump directly to the objective of the game by choosing to lower your waterline and getting real. When you do, you will begin the process of healing your core wounds and awakening to Love-Based-Consciousness.

*Did I hear you right? Are you saying that God* **wants** *us to suffer?*

God most emphatically does not *want* you to suffer. God does not *want* anything. God simply *is*. Wanting implies duality, someone wanting and that which is desired. God contains all of duality, all possible "isness," yet does not identify with any of it. If you choose to suffer, then God-As-Us is exploring all that suffering has to offer. Remember that you *are* God. You created this game *for you* to play, so God-As-Us could experience life *through* you.

Whether or not you suffer, you will continue to be God. When your body dies, the illusion of separation drops away and you become fully conscious of your Divinity, along with the knowledge of what it has meant to experience this life. You will also participate in a fabulous cast party, but that's a story for a later chapter.

So, the real question is, do you want to suffer? If so, that is always available. You can hang on to your core wounds, defend your choice to be right at all costs, cast yourself as the ultimate victim, wallow in fear and make your life as miserable as you like. Just be aware that suffering is optional, *not* mandatory. You can always choose to leave suffering behind.

*Now I'm really confused. If I can't control the events of my life, how can I possibly choose to stop suffering?*

Suffering has different aspects. Remember Viktor Frankl? He had no control over the events of his imprisonment and torture by the Nazis, but he found that he did have control over what he made his experiences mean. He chose not to let his suffering overwhelm him. Though his body must have been wracked with pain, and his mind with doubt and fear, by consciously choosing compassion his spirit remained vibrantly alive. If he could make that choice in those circumstances, do you really doubt that you can choose compassion in your life? His example makes clear that though you may be physically and emotionally suffering, your spirit can still soar.

Of course, most of the people in Mr. Frankl's situation died in abject fear. We wish to emphasize that *every single time* a person dies violently, whether by the sword, arrows, spears, knives or bullets, the fear is excruciating. You are hardwired to fear death way down in the amygdala. That's what panic is all about.

Let us be clear, however. Most of you in the developed world do not regularly face the stark reality of imminent death, though being immersed in a world soaked in violence and supported by sensational media does create stress in your bodies that causes your health to deteriorate in very real ways.

A recent study by the University of Maryland Medical Center[31] demonstrates conclusively that watching comedies increases blood flow an average of 22%, while watching disturbing, violent movies constricts blood vessels and decreases blood flow an average of 35%. A decrease in blood flow equals an increase in blood pressure, with less oxygen delivered to each cell.

We find it fascinating to note that this occurs even in people who claim to be unaffected by watching violence. Though they may feel nothing consciously, their bodies are still stressed. Stress is insidious in your culture, and it is taking such a toll that it's beginning to decrease your average life span. The twin epidemics of morbid obesity and diabetes only begin to hint at the looming health crisis.

*What are you talking about? I recently read that our average lifespan is longer than ever.*

Many of the sickest people, including the homeless, are simply not included in morbidity statistics. Many more are counted under categories that make it seem as though you are healthier than ever. Statistics do seem to bear out that you are indeed living longer. The sad truth is that the warehouses of the dying that you call nursing homes are filled to overflowing with worn-out husks, bodies which are no longer occupied, their souls having long since fled this place for Home. This is one of the ways that longevity statistics are manipulated to make it seem as though your health is improving. It is not.

Can you see the death spiral your culture is locked into? Your stressful world affords you endless opportunities to self-medicate. Highly processed foods, alcohol, drugs, work, TV, sex, they're all unhealthy when used in excess. Culturally, you are taught that you are not good enough, and then aggressively sold products and services you are told will make you feel better. In reality, what you buy often makes you feel worse. And around and around you go, chained firmly to the hamster wheel of FBC.

*Is it ever really possible, then, to heal my core wounds? Aren't some of them so basic to my personality that they're an inextricable part of who I am?*

Once you are willing to take this inquiry of "who I am" far enough, you will come to understand that your personality has nothing whatsoever to do with who you really are. As many teachers, including Gangaji and Ramana Maharshi, have said, you are existance itself. It is out of this existance, or "isness," that all things, including personalities, manifest. While your essence cannot be wounded in any way, wounds often form the core of the pearl of personality. To let go of those wounds is to die, at least in some sense, to who we thought we were.

Again, the answer lies in being present. As long as any core wound runs you, you will experience everything and everyone in the context of that wound. This aspect of your "self" or "personality" is a construct of your ego to rationalize your wounding. Even though this aspect is also always God, it is so anchored in its wounds that it colors everything that happens to you through that lens, at least as long as you remain unconscious of it.

# Drunk with Wonder

# 37 Guess Who's in Charge?

Just as a wave on the ocean is what the ocean is doing, you are what God is doing.
– *Wayne Dyer*

With this in mind, guess who's in charge of your stories? You are! You get to choose anew what each event of your life does or does not mean. Only this time, you have the benefit of a far more informed perspective, as well as an understanding that you, and only you, have the power to make these choices.

*I'm feeling both terrified and excited about all of this. I know, I know, you don't have to say it. I just need to breathe and stay present.*

Perfect! You've got it. Now, just stay present with your breath as you allow the fear to dissipate, and let us continue.

Another crucial point further defines what we mean by healing core wounds. We are not suggesting that healing requires that they disappear from your memory. Though your wounds will always be the grains of sand around which coalesce the pearl of your personality, they will no longer run your life.

For example, separation anxiety is one core experience that everyone shares. This is another of the primal emotions we have been speaking about. We bring it up again because of its central theme in what it means to the human experience. No matter how perfect your gestation, how much you are loved, how peaceful your birth, separation anxiety is triggered when you leave your mother's womb. Once the umbilical cord is cut and you can no longer feel your mother's pulse, your entrance onto "the stage of life" crystallizes the seed of your separate self.

Remember, in Western society it is a common practice to leave babies alone to cry themselves to sleep in their cribs. You do this ostensibly to toughen them so they don't become "spoiled," so they'll learn they can't get whatever they want whenever they want it. Whatever the merits of this idea (and we submit that there are none), the result has been to create individuals who may indeed be tough.

In this case, though, tough simply means emotionally numb, as evidenced by your mastery at distracting yourselves from your feelings. Sadly, many parents leave their babies crying merely to pursue selfish interests. They just can't be bothered, or it simply isn't convenient. This conditioning has been a direct precursor to creating a culture where toughness and the concomitant ability to inflict emotional and physical pain onto others are valued.

*It makes me crazy when I hear a baby crying helplessly. It's so sad!*

We feel your compassionate heart shining through, and we gratefully bask in the warmth of your love. Notice that when you consciously breathe into your compassion, your heart opens further.

Recent research shows that many of a new-born baby's neuronal connections have yet to be formed. While trillions of these pathways are available at birth, every experience that a baby has results in some of those pathways being pruned away, while others become stronger. This happens at a prodigious rate, especially during the first two years of life. This wiring is powerfully influenced by the baby's environment. After all, aren't emotions often triggered by bodily experiences?

Conversely, emotions can trigger bodily responses. As a baby, you aren't able to differentiate between them, so they are perceived as one and the same. Babies don't have a clue about manipulation and control except, "If I cry and get fed, changed, held and loved, then I have worth. If I cry and don't get cared for, then I am *not* worthy."

*Now I understand why babies would feel that way.*

Exactly. We submit that this is the *core* of low self-esteem. While later life experiences can reinforce these early lessons, it is here that your brains become programmed with the particular filters, or stories, that you use to create meaning out of the "isness." A baby quickly learns whether its cries are effective at satisfying its need to be fed, changed, held and loved unconditionally. These become the foundational stories upon which your sense of self-worth, or lack of it, is based. If these needs are not met, you quickly learn hopelessness.

Even when given food, warmth and shelter, a baby can still wither and even die if its emotional needs, including the all-important element of touch, are not met.[32] That's how a baby knows it's loved. It's not thinking yet, it's feeling. If its feelings are not honored and respected, it sinks into lethargy, which ultimately leads to depression. We now know that depression runs in families, and is commonly thought to be gene-based in many cases.

Researchers are looking for a magic pill to "cure" depression, instead of considering whether the brain abnormalities they are seeing might be from early childhood experiences of neglect and abuse. These are traits which also run in families, being passed on from parent to child. That's how your culture perpetuates abuse. It is learned behavior! A healthy, deeply loved child does not wake up one day and randomly decide to harm another. It is *learned* behavior!

## Impossible Trails

Impossible trails
Broken through
Trackless wilderness

Whole continents
Long ago
Abandoned to fear
Reclaimed as
Sacred ground

Hearts breaking open
Spilling tears
Like dreams
Flooding Earth
With new beginnings –

# 38 The Triune Brain

> We still do not know one ten-thousandth of one percent of what nature has revealed to us.
>
> – *Albert Einstein*

*I'm curious as to how your teachings correspond with the results of scientific research into the physiology and psychology of the brain.*

It turns out that what you have is, in reality, a triune brain. There are three separate and distinct physical structures, each vibrating at its own set of frequencies and providing a different piece of the puzzle. By far the largest, and also the newest from an evolutionary perspective, is the neocortex, also known as the cerebral cortex, where language, higher reasoning and complex analytical processes are conducted.

Within the cerebral cortex lies the mid-brain, also known as the mammalian brain or limbic system, which creates and processes feelings such as affection, mood, and motivation. The most basic of the three, the reptilian brain, which you know as the instinctual brain, lies cocooned within these two brains. Perched on top of the spinal column, it is responsible for autonomic bodily functions including heartbeat, breathing, temperature, digestion and so forth.

*Until you mentioned it earlier, I never realized that part of my brain had a reptilian origin. Does that mean I'm related to, or even think like, a komodo dragon or an alligator?*

While not recently related, the relationship is there, especially in how your autonomic nervous system reacts to your environment. Thankfully, though, you have other parts of your brain that allow you to mediate the raw data through your consciousness. By doing so, you have the ability to access the stories around your core wounds, allowing you to heal them if you choose to embark on what may, at first, appear to be a most frightening path.

Our teaching is that as you venture out of the neocortex into deeper areas of the brain, you move away from the familiar world of thought and language into a feeling world that can seem not just unfamiliar, but downright terrifying. Within your culture you actively avoid exploring these areas. Many of you have even been taught that the subconscious is where the devil dwells. Part of our teaching is that this is actually where fear, superstition and ignorance thrive and fester.

What is usually called evil is actually the outward expression of great emotional pain and trauma. Though we in no way condone cruelty or violence, it's crucial to compassionately comprehend what lies at the root of such heinous acts. To truly transform your world, you must embrace your disowned parts and hold each other close as you heal. As long as even one person on Earth doesn't feel safe, none of you will truly be safe.

When you identify and lovingly confront your core wounds, you move below the surface of your consciousness. Though there is still much you do not yet fully comprehend, it seems clear that the conscious mind roughly corresponds to the neocortex, while the subconscious is directly linked to the mammalian and reptilian parts of your brain.

As we have previously discussed, science has identified the most primitive emotions that reside deep within the mammalian brain known as the amygdala. They include panic, rage, separation anxiety, lust (sexual desire) and seeking. These are all clearly related to survival, and when they are activated, either by an imminent threat or a perceived opportunity for procreation, they have the ability to overpower all but the most focused control of the neocortex.

*I know that when I'm sexually aroused, every other thought seems to vanish. Is this what you're talking about?*

That's certainly part of it. The most basic instincts around sex, naturally, are to procreate at all costs. From the perspective of evolution, nothing is more crucial than passing on your genes. Even though your culture chooses not to look at it this way, it is obvious that almost everything you do, from the clothes you wear to the cars you drive, are elaborate displays meant to communicate your sexual desirability to potential mates. Keeping the body alive long enough to procreate helps assure continuation of the species, so when your very lives are at stake, rage or panic can serve as powerful survival mechanisms.

*You make it sound as though evolution cares only about procreation. It sounds pretty cold-blooded to me.*

That's the reptile in you. Remember, reptiles literally are cold-blooded. At their level, survival of the species is not personal. In setting up the game, God-As-Us has clearly shown, to say the least, an interesting sense of humor.

*Interesting? You got that right! Since you brought it up, what do you think of sex?*

Well, we're all for it! Seriously, it is obviously one of the most sublime experiences people could ever share with each other. Quite aside from the procreational benefits, sharing our bodies in such an intimate way is one of the great miracles of life. Now, having said that, we wish to make it extremely clear that we do not condone any form of sexual activity that is not entirely mutually consensual. We believe that all sex should be safe, and that condoms and birth control are vital components of safety. We strongly and unequivocally support a woman's right to choose. It is *her* body. Your body is *your* temple. If someone chooses not to have an abortion, that is their right. They *do not*, however, have the right to force another not to have one.

Furthermore, we feel that the current hysteria around same-sex unions is a perfect example of Fear-Based-Consciousness in action. People who love each other, who want to share their lives, are nothing short of miracles in action. As a culture, you need to, once and for all, get out of each other's bedrooms. Don't just tolerate diversity, celebrate it!

*I'm delighted to hear you say that. I have several gay friends, and I love them dearly. It's absurd for people to be so afraid of them, to think they're out to corrupt our youth.*

We understand, and simply ask you to remember compassion. Those who are this fear-filled have been wounded by their own families and culture, traumatized by stories that are simply not true. Love is love. It is not gender based.

And speaking of youth, can you see how you live in a sexualized society? You tell your youth that abstinence is best while simultaneously bombarding them with sex-soaked media. You all know that sexual hormones are raging when you are young, and that expressing those drives can feel like riding fireworks straight to heaven. With no education, especially around your emotions, most often those experiences cause more pain than celebration. But telling young people to "Just say no" is like telling the sun not to shine. As a culture, you need to come to grips with the "isness" of your sexuality in all its flavors and permutations, and find wise, responsible ways to educate your youth so that they make healthy choices around every aspect of their lives, including their bodies.

*All I can say about that is, where the heck were you when I was a teenager?*

As close as your breath, dear one. You just hadn't learned to listen to your own Higher Self yet. For now, though, let us continue with our discussion of the triune brain.

Scientific research shows quite clearly that these three areas of the brain are largely self-contained, with far more neural pathways within each individual structure than there are connecting them. This understanding of the brain goes a long way towards explaining why you can feel so incredibly stuck after getting triggered into these primal emotions.

Since birth, you have been meticulously trained to mistrust your instincts. This natural wildness, when disowned, can get you into trouble. Ironically, these same instincts also hold the key to your deepest passions and most potent energies. Imagine these unfelt feelings stuffed in a balloon. They become largely self-contained, with limited cortical connections between them and the rest of your brain. Your primal emotions are mediated first through your reptilian brain, then through your limbic system, and finally through the cerebral cortex.

The instinctual brain sits directly on top of the spinal column. This is a perfect place from which to direct the body's autonomic functions. Signals are transferred instantly to the central nervous system, bypassing the higher centers of the brain. As we've seen, this allows virtually instantaneous reactions (fight or flight) in any situation. By the time these instinctual emotions have reached the cerebral cortex, your stories have thoroughly obscured their "below the waterline" origins.

*I'm seeing more and more clearly how strongly my earliest memories continue to affect me. In this moment, just thinking about them, I'm feeling my heart beginning to race.*

You're doing a great job noticing your feelings. Know you are safe, and notice your heartbeat slow as you continue to breathe.

Another useful way of looking at all of this is through the context of body, mind, heart and spirit. Exploring this perspective, we start with the body's five senses, which pass information from your environment through the physical structure of your nervous system into your brain. The mind, which seems to be generated through the biochemical functioning of your brain's neuronal connections, filters this information through the context of your stories. Your heart is the home of emotional responses and motivations referred to as feelings. Finally, we come to spirit, which we suggest is the synergistic weaving of the other three. Your ego, your relationship with self and others, and the intangible essence that connects your brains to the Infinite, all dance together in this miracle we call life.

We can now see that there is a relatively narrow conduit between your thinking mind and your reptilian brain. When your brain gets triggered it feels as though a trap door has opened and you've fallen into a maelstrom of poisonous emotions, a place of such intense suffering that your one desire is to escape by any means possible. We assure you that there are many healthy ways to climb out of this toxic morass. These positive pathways are far different than culturally approved numbing agents you have used, including alcohol, drugs, violence, sex, TV and work.

Becoming aware of these neuronal pathways can, in and of itself, be a huge revelation. However, you must also be willing to stop flailing about in order to find the ladder of consciousness you need to extricate yourself from the pit of despair and return to the peace and serenity of love-based awareness. One of our greatest teachings holds that by consciously breathing into and through your fear, you can relax enough to remember the way Home. We say again: **Fear is excitement without breath.**

# 39 Escaping from the Pit of Despair

> Take the riskiest path you can find. What looks like the safe path is an illusion. What looks like a risk is an illusion. Take the riskiest path you can find.
> – *Caroline Myss*

*I do recognize this dark place you're referring to. It gives me the shivers just thinking about it. It's probably the scariest place I know. I hate it there!*

We hear you, dear one. Finding a way out is no doubt the single greatest challenge many people ever face. A significant component of the pharmaceutical industry, not to mention the adult beverage business, is devoted to alleviating the agony of this black hole. Perhaps you've found a more positive way to get out of that place.

*I have found that going to the gym for a workout really helps give me a major attitude adjustment. Is that what you mean?*

Absolutely! Physical activity, including sports, can be a tremendous release and grounding tool, especially when used consciously. Numerous body-centered therapies are based upon this wisdom, and can often assist the healing process.

While many activities and spiritual practices can help you break out of this pit of despair (and we highly encourage their responsible use), we teach that in order to create an ongoing peace inside, a deep exploration of the shadow side is required. Over time, you can consciously choose to create new neuronal pathways between the different sections of the brain, thus integrating them into a seamless whole. This results in becoming triggered much less frequently.

By continuously reinforcing these new choices, you can reprogram your habitual patterns, detoxifying old stories by processing emotions in a healthy, positive way. When you've completed this phase of your healing, and continue emptying your balloon and keeping your waterline lowered, there is little toxic sludge to get triggered into. You can then honor and respect your memories in a healthy way, pay attention to your inner wisdom, and experience yourself as whole.

These instinct-based emotional states clearly have a profound influence on your entire world, in part because you so often deny their effects or attribute them to something else. Terrorists, the Devil, Infidels, Republicans, Democrats, even Karma, can all appear to be outside forces, which potently serve to keep you stuck in the familiar role of victim.

*What you're saying is pretty intense. I mean, how can there be no victims? I see victims everywhere. War, famine, earthquakes, floods, tsunamis, crooks and politicians all seem to produce helpless, innocent victims.*

They do indeed, though we suggest that "seem to" is the operative term here. If you wish to play the role of victim, there is no shortage of casting calls. Just remember that if you choose to live from the victim role (and it is a choice, whether you believe it or not), you are helpless to change your condition. In order to create different circumstances, you must be willing to give up the victim role and take charge of your experience. For example, instead of wringing your hands and saying that the hurricane (or the fire, or the flood) destroyed your life, choose to see the hurricane as a gift to help you do your life differently. As long as you see yourself as a victim, someone else is in charge. If you're in charge, then you have choices. Which do you prefer?

Which brings us back to "Them and Us." Those who seek power learn many ways to manipulate others. As long as the masses remain ignorant of these issues, those in control can safely remain there, using their well-ensconced power to do whatever they want. They have created a meta-story that makes your instinctual drives wrong, and those who succumb to the power of these drives are labeled as bad or evil.

Sex, for instance, is used to sell everything from booze to cigarettes, cars to car wax, clothing to perfume. Yet the act of sex is held as being dirty or perverted unless it's performed in the context of a hetero-sexual marriage, preferably to conceive progeny. Having sex simply to express affection, joy, ecstacy or perhaps celebrating the miracle of life is taught by many religions to be the work of the devil. Hence the rabid intensity with which some people judge others who do not choose, for whatever reason, to fit into those narrow strictures. Our teaching is that whatever mutually consenting adults do in the privacy of their own homes is no one's business but their own.

At the same time that those in power are stridently shouting about how sin-filled the peons are, they flout the same strictures they demand others live by. In this regard, we mention Richard Nixon, Jerry Falwell, Jimmy Swagert, Jim and Tammy Fae Baker, Bill Clinton, Martha Stewart, Ken Lay of Enron, John Rigas and his son Tim of Adelphia Cable, former WorldCom Inc. CEO Bernard Ebbers, and what seems at times to be the entire current administration and much of congress. These are but a few examples of the, "Power corrupts, and absolute power corrupts absolutely,"[33] school of FBC. History is replete with those who say something to the effect of, "Do what we say, not what we do."

It is *precisely* when the masses discover that they've been had by those in control that revolution occurs. Though they operate by different rules, don't you find it ironic that those in power have been as much at the mercy of their deep emotional drives as the rest of you?

*It sure doesn't look that way from here. Many times I've wished I had the power I've seen others wielding, and wondered, "Why them and not me?"*

Perhaps because you are choosing a higher path. Although all paths are meaningful at some level, your choice to participate in this book, at this time, shows an awareness blossoming within you. Fear is the driver towards external power, and when you live in fear and lack there is *never* enough. We believe you are becoming aware of this truth right in this moment. Remember that it was your parents, teachers and other authority figures who taught you to fear these drives. Because you've learned to keep your instincts below the waterline, you tend to remain unaware of and therefore helpless to their vicissitudes.

When you were little, your emotions were much closer to the surface and you acted them out. Screaming, throwing tantrums, laughing hysterically, exploring forbidden realms such as your own body, all may have been tolerated to a limited degree, until you were old enough to "know better." Then you were told to "act your age," that "big boys don't cry," to "not be a girl," perhaps that "girls shouldn't sweat," and our favorite, "stop crying or I'll give you something to cry about!" You obeyed or else, though often feeling great resentment and anger in doing so.

Separation anxiety is another of these primal emotions we've been talking about. This deeply-rooted anxiety is readily apparent in the hysteria young children experience when they are separated from their parents as they are dropped off at school for the first time. In the often fragmented culture you live in, many people spend their lives feeling lost and alone. It's a leading cause of suicide.

Libido (or seeking, as it's referred to in this context), which is the last of the primal emotions we've been speaking of, accounts for the deep urge to see what is over the next hill. It drives new discoveries, conquests, understanding the world, your origins and even God. Libido, as seeking, fuels your insatiable curiosity.

So, with no tools to deal with your emotions in a healthy way, you find yourself in a world where hundreds of thousands of people are slaughtered every year, and sexual assault and rape are epidemic. You have road rage, sports rage, racial and ethnic rage, religious rage and much, much more. It is clear that the core instincts of fight or flight are essentially identical to rage and panic.

*I understand what you're suggesting, and heaven knows I have a healthy sex drive, but I've never remotely considered rape or slaughter. And I hardly ever think about suicide any more, though I often feel alone. I just thought it was part of the human condition. I guess I'm not getting how all these feelings are connected to our primal emotions.*

Your feelings and your primal emotions are one and the same. The apaprent difference consists only of a patina of stories laid down by family, culture and religion. Let us take another look at some of these emotions, and perhaps the connection will become clearer.

Your sexual drive got you in trouble on more than one occasion, especially when you were a teenager. Though you certainly never raped anyone, your raging hormones made you do some pretty crazy things. Perhaps you can appreciate how some people, with no skills in dealing with their emotions, might "step over the line" and harm another. Rape, in the context of the reptilian brain, can be seen as acting out your profoundly instinctual sexual drive, which is inextricably linked to the biological imperative to reproduce at all costs. In modern society, rape (which we define as forcing one's self sexually on another against their will) though sometimes motivated from a different perspective, is often the abuse of power rather than a desire to pass on one's genes. In either case rape still originates from inappropriately expressing primal emotions.

It is interesting to note that the overwhelming majority of people who commit rape were themselves raped, usually at an early age and often repeatedly. People raised in a healthy, loving environment just don't get up one morning and decide to rape someone. That rape is so common in your culture does not mean it is inherent, or instinctual, in nature. Rape is primarily *learned* behavior.

To sum up this conversation about primitive emotions: your body releases intoxicating levels of adrenaline when it is triggered by either a real or perceived threat. Remember, adrenaline is perhaps the most addictive substance you've ever known. In your fast-paced society, virtually everyone exhibits symptoms of adrenaline addiction. In its milder forms, you find yourself craving vicarious thrills often satisfied by watching endless amounts of television, including sports, action movies, and "reality" TV. In its more advanced forms, it shows up in everything from watching violent, gore-drenched movies to aggressive driving (and the related appeal for lots of horsepower and sporty cars).

Those who hunger for an even more intense rush may participate in extreme sports, unsafe sex, binge drinking, drinking and driving, smoking, killing animals for sport, shooting drugs, fighting, rape, torture and murder.

There is perhaps no greater adrenaline rush than war, which is a major reason so many of your young people still volunteer. The subject of war brings us back to what appears to be humanity's favorite story, that of the small band fighting against insurmountable odds, as evidenced by how often you retell it in its endless permutations.

*Wow! You make adrenaline sound incredibly dangerous.*

Consistently fatal, actually. But the more you know about its effects on the body and your addiction to it, the more you get to choose your relationship with it. There is much to be explored and more deeply understood in this arena. Science has not yet figured out all of your instinctual drives. Not by a long shot!

And, even though many researchers have attempted to develop models to explain, in evolutionary terms, feelings of altruism for family, friends, tribe and community, these models have not yet demonstrated that such feelings are entirely instinctual. Clearly, there is also a mothering or care-giving instinct as well as nesting behavior. Then, of course, love is an incredibly powerful emotion that can sweep you off your feet, intoxicating you to the point of behaving like a fool, at least from the perspective of those who are not also in love at the time.

Your subconscious drives, encoded in your very DNA, have played a necessary role in getting you this far. As a culture, you have made some of these drives wrong, acting as if you can physically pound ethics and morality into each other. And while people can indeed be terrified into behaving in ways that please their rulers, it inevitably creates resentment, which stokes rage, which fuels rebellion, which has led to war countless times throughout your history. The result? Those who triumph over their oppressors usually begin the cycle all over again, taking revenge on their overlords, creating resentment, and on around the hamster wheel you go.

We invite you to join us in calling for emotional literacy and the greatly enhanced awareness such a perspective can engender. It is only when you have a thorough context within which you can deeply grok your human condition that you will begin to heal. As we've seen, true healing requires compassionate understanding and acceptance of all parts of yourself. You don't have to be at the mercy of your hormones and the wild mood swings they can cause, but you will certainly continue to be as long as you deny your instinct-rich origins.

Drunk with Wonder

# 40 The Precious Pearl Revisited

Life is a banquet. And the tragedy is that most people are starving to death.
–*Anthony de Mello*

*Will healing my core wounds help me gain control of my emotions?*

Yes, and the first step is awareness, which is where most people miss the boat. They have somehow convinced themselves that if they work hard enough at ignoring their core wounds, they will eventually go away. Of course, as we've already discussed, this idea denies the fundamental nature of core wounds. To access your core wounds, you must follow the path of their entry, usually through your body and mind to your heart and spirit. By definition, a core wound is one that touches all four.

Remember, we teach that these wounds are like grains of sand caught in oysters. Just as the oyster creates a pearl that surrounds the sand grain to keep it from cutting more deeply into its delicate flesh, you can re-frame your wounds to help you foster Love-Based-Consciousness. Re-framing your wounds allows you to heal so that you may refashion your personality into one that is more compassionate, peaceful and joy-filled. Your ego-based personality does not have to be destroyed in order to support an enlightened life. You can honor your wounds, just as they are, with love and respect.

You can incorporate all of it, including the suffering you experienced before you realized it was optional, into your pearl. Just remember that you wouldn't want to allow your fear-based personality to run your life any more than you would allow a beloved pearl necklace to do so. Instead, use the wisdom you can glean from grokking the teachings of your wounds to create loving, nurturing and understanding relationships with everyone, starting with yourself.

*That's a beautiful metaphor. Thank you for your patient and gentle guidance. I am profoundly grateful.*

You're quite welcome. We see you working so very diligently on this goal, and we honor your commitment. And now, it is time to more fully face your ego.

## Drunk with Wonder

Drunk with wonder
I gaze at the wild,
Lustrous pearl
Of my personality
Shining in the center
Of the One Heart
Like a candle flame
In the heart of the sun
And know my Source
My Destination -
When I let go of knowing
I become the sun
Assume the crown
Of creation
And am Home –

# 41 Embracing the Ego

We need not create heaven on earth,
But rather quiet ourselves
So that we may know it is already here.
– *Franklin Markowitz*

Certain spiritual traditions believe that ego is the ultimate enemy, and claim that you must kill it if you ever want to achieve enlightenment. We do not see it this way. Your ego is not a problem to be solved; it is a useful, even essential ally on the journey through life. If you choose to tell yourself a different story, such as egos need to be ruthlessly controlled, or even that they are bad and must be eliminated, you will create a great deal of drama in your life, since your ego has a powerful capacity for self-defense.

It has been our experience that egos not fully conscious of their role in the drama often create all kinds of havoc in the manifest world. The ego is a virtual construct of thoughts, feelings and beliefs. It is nothing more or less than a unique collection of stories. Take away the stories, and nothing remains. The context of these stories contain a past full of ancestors, family history, self-history and cultural history. Though your ego is terrified of death, in the end there is nothing to fear. All that is lost is the limited perspective your fear-based ego holds. We find it rather ironic that when the ego "lives" in terror, the soul connected to it cannot fully appreciate the exquisite ecstasy of life.

*But if my ego is wrapped around my core wounds like a pearl around a grain of sand, doesn't that mean I have to overcome my ego in order to heal them?*

This dance is a central paradox of life, one that is vital to contemplate. The more you resist your ego, the harder it fights to survive. That's why those who seek to destroy their own egos must inevitably experience a tremendous struggle, as they are quite literally locked in a life and death battle with themselves. If, however, you accept your ego as a natural and vital part of your self, and enlist it in your quest for enlightenment, your journey will be much easier and far more attainable, not to mention way more fun.

Liberation from suffering simply means resting in pure awareness, floating in the infinite sea of no mind, though it may appear to others that no one is home to enjoy it. The ego/mind wants life to be harder, for it to be an epic journey, to win the prize against overwhelming odds. And since there are an infinite number of opportunities to experience grand adventures, filled with casts of good guys, bad guys, awesome locations and outrageous special effects, the ego has ample opportunity to experience all of it.

By setting aside your preconceptions and simply allowing yourself to see the "isness" clearly, you come to understand there is nothing but perfection in the universe, as there is nothing but God/Goddess every where and every when. Surrendering your identification with your body, job, various roles, money and all that you attach to these things is essential to resting in the boundless ocean of joy.

From this place of Oneness all experiences flow, and then inevitably return. The great in-breath and out-breath of God, the eternal heartbeat of the One, is what you experience as the repeated incarnation of individual life. In some traditions, this story is seen as a trap from which it is life's ultimate purpose to escape. Getting off the karmic wheel of birth and death is seen as the goal, and so it's not surprising to see the suffering of so many who believe in this story.

*Well, I started this dialogue thinking that reincarnation was no more than superstition, and now I'm not so sure. I certainly hope that if I do come back again I will do so with more insight than I did this time.*

We see that you are quickly gaining an appreciation of this perspective, and the deeper truth is that there is truly nowhere you can go and nothing you can do that will bring you any closer to God than you are right here, right now. Why? Because any experience of separation is illusion. There is no one here but God experiencing the Self. You don't have to get off the great wheel, or meditate for some number of years, or flog yourself with chains, or say some number of Hail Mary's, or anything else. All that is necessary is to let go of the belief that there is anything called separation, and rest in pure awareness with no story, no mind and no suffering. As we've said before, it's not that suffering is somehow wrong or bad, because that is God, too, but what an amazing realization to grok down to the bone that suffering is optional!

Allow yourself to feel the deliciously rich connections that weave the universe together, and the profound perfection in which it floats. Let go of all worries, for there is no one and no thing to worry about. No fear, as there is no lack. Nothing (no thing) wrong, as the universe is always perfectly itself. Experience each moment as perfection, and simply accept that there is nothing to fix.

The immeasurable gift of creation is available with each breath. An infinite supply of unconditional love, joy and peace is always available whenever you choose to surrender your stories to the contrary. This infinite field of pure potential is nothing less than the limitless ocean of joy the masters speak of.

The ego is not some wicked aberration that needs to be tamed or killed. In fact, according to some wisdom traditions, there is truly no ego to kill in the first place, for when you mount an inquiry into the ego/mind it all dissolves into an illusory mist of stories, contexts, labels and histories. Your ego may feel real, in that it has experiences, thoughts, feelings and relationships, or at least thinks it does, but there's the key…thinking.

When thoughts are observed rising and falling like waves on the beach, you can directly experience that you are not only the wave, you're the ocean out of which all waves spring. When you choose to identify with a given wave, you tend to become attached to the attributes (or stories) of that wave. When you choose to rest in the ocean of who you really are, then infinite resources of love, light, joy and peace are always available, as you will have surrendered any limiting beliefs that you are less than whole.

*Frankly, what you're describing seems too easy. Surely there's more to enlightenment than this.*

Your ego wants to feel as though you have been through an epic struggle against overwhelming odds, which, of course, it can then take full credit for. Of course, this is a manifestation of your scarcity story, the one that believes you can't ever have something without struggling for it, or else you won't deserve it. To put that one to rest, go outside and watch a sunset, then ask yourself, what could you ever "do" to deserve such beauty? Reflect on the awareness that you *are* God, and that as God, you created everything that is. Now ask yourself: what more are you required to do to be deserving of the abundance of this creation?

Finally, simply surrender to a larger perspective than can be contained in any individual mind, and give yourself credit for getting out of your own way. Wake up to *Who You Really Are* in this now moment. You are nothing less than a Divine manifestation of God, making up all of creation, moment by moment. Do you want to continue making it up out of fear? Do you want to continue to experience suffering, whether it be your own or another's? Recognize that right now and *only* right now, you are completely free to choose how you will experience this moment.

## 42 Pain is Inevitable, Suffering is Optional

> Pain is a relatively objective, physical phenomenon; suffering is our psychological resistance to what happens. Events may create physical pain, but they do not in themselves create suffering. Resistance creates suffering. Stress happens when your mind resists what is....The only problem in your life is your mind's resistance to life as it unfolds.
>
> – *Dan Millman*

*Whenever I've really focused on being present, I have been able, at least for a moment, to completely surrender and simply rest in the ocean of joy. I start to experience euphoria, and then suddenly I feel overwhelmed by fear. I feel myself shaking just thinking about it. What is that all about?*

It's common to be so invested in your stories that your ego feels as though it will literally die if you let go of your fear and victim-based perspective. This is not Truth, it is simply another story. You've spent your whole life learning how to interpret the "isness" a certain way. Now, in the time it has taken you to participate in the creation of this book, you have learned that you are have many exciting choices. Give yourself time and keep practicing. If you truly want what we've been describing, it is totally available in this moment. Remember that you have been lost in the drama, an unknowing player in the greatest of all passion plays, and you are just beginning to awaken.

Much of what some refer to as Enlightenment is simply becoming grounded in this truth, knowing in your bones that you are a perfect expression of God right here and right now. From this perspective, suffering is understood as the feeling you have when you resist the "isness" of the Now.

*I've always thought of suffering as something that happens to me, but now I see that I actually create my own suffering. It's my interpretation of events, rather than the events themselves, that creates my suffering. The hardest part for me seems to be around becoming aware the moment I start to suffer, and then to have the courage to make a more loving choice.*

We understand. Trust that it will become easier over time. For now, consider this example: Imagine that you fell and scraped your knee. In the past, you might have felt clumsy and created suffering out of judging yourself as wrong or bad for being such a klutz. But the "isness" is simply that you scraped your knee. It bled, it stung, it hurt, it was bruised and sore. That's it! That's the "isness" of the moment...a bruised, sore, scraped, bleeding knee. In not making yourself wrong by, for example, excoriating yourself for scraping it, you can experience the considerable grace of no suffering. Because you aren't resisting the moment, you simply notice the pain, accept it for what it is, and go on to the next moment. By not beating yourself up over the experience, you eliminate suffering as a consequence.

You're so conditioned in this world to put the words pain and suffering together that they often sound like "painandsuffering." You often hear about the pain and suffering clause in lawsuits, but what we are speaking of here is not the same thing at all. Pain is physical, suffering is emotional. Pain is inevitable, suffering is optional. Does this help your understanding?

*Yes, I'm beginning to see how I've confused pain with suffering.*

Wonderful! Now you can see why we have spent so much time on this subject. In choosing to surrender, the ego can let go of the belief that

it has to suffer in order to be. Can the ego still be without suffering? If you believe it can't, that is one story, and if you believe it can, that is another. Remember, it's *all* story. It's truly your choice in each now moment whether to hold that, "I suffer, therefore I am," or that "I am," free of suffering.

# 43 Jumping off the Cliff of Your Fears

> The human species is engaged in a major transformation. Through the human species, the universe is becoming conscious of itself.
>
> – *Robert Muller*

Keep in mind that you're making *all* of it up, *all* of the time. There is the "isness" of the moment, and then there is your collection of stories that gives meaning and context to the "isness." You can choose from literally an infinite number of stories as to what, if any, meaning there may be, but in reality you are God pretending you are not. In each moment, the stories you choose perfectly reflect whether you are living in Fear-Based or Love-Based-Consciousness.

You may experience your ego moving towards healing and then running away, as though testing you to see if your self-love is truly unconditional, checking repeatedly to see if you can trust you. It is as though you are determined to discover how lost in fear you can become and still feel lovable. Can you see that this dance between intimacy and running away is exactly what we go through in our relationships with others, including parents, lovers, children and friends?

*What do you mean, "To see if I can trust me?"*

It's absolutely a trust issue, the deepest one anyone will ever face. In fact, before you can ever trust anyone else, you must first learn to trust yourself. So, do you trust yourself to face your own ego, to take on your

core wounds, no matter how much you would rather leave them alone? Do you trust yourself to forgive all the people in your life who you thought did you wrong, especially those who you felt abandoned you, and whose victimization you've been clinging to? Do you trust enough to forgive yourself for whatever suffering you have experienced as a result of not knowing that suffering is optional? Do you trust yourself to throw open the door to abundance, love, peace and joy in your life? Do you trust yourself to take the first step by lowering your waterline with yourself?

*You call it a first step, but it feels huge, like jumping off a cliff.*

We know. It is a cliff, the cliff of your fears. For all practical purposes, it is the highest cliff in the universe.

*I'm not sure what to do.*

The truth is that it is not about *doing*. It is about *being*. You don't need to do anything in order to prove your worth, because you have always been priceless. Simply being is enough. Just allow yourself to be the God that you already are. After that, the doing will take care of itself.

*So, how do I go about lowering my waterline?*

Become vulnerable. Choose to be authentic about what you feel in this now moment, starting with yourself. Then find someone whom you experience as particularly conscious and ask for their help in becoming more conscious. Or, if that's too big a step, start journaling.[34] Consider attending a workshop or retreat in your area.[35]

Remember, it's all God, all the time. In the blink of an eye, in the time it takes for your heart to beat, you will find that all the vaunted treasures of Heaven are right here, right now, inside you.

# Beyond Separation

Out of the darkness and despair of delusion
Beyond the loneliness of pain and separation

We soar triumphant into the crystal skies
Of a new world where no one dies

And everyone has let go of their pain,
Deciding we were too tired to remain

Locked away behind our illusory walls
Or stalking unsuspecting egos down endless halls

Leading back in circles to the drama
Of learning that our belief in Karma

Keeps us stuck in the dance
Awaiting some half-imagined chance

To break free and finally own
Our mastery right down to the bone

And let go of a past that no longer suits us
Take off the costumes that starve us

Of the light and love shining down from above,
Take up our true nature as conscious co-creators

Jump off the cliff of our fears
And fly away Home –

Drunk with Wonder

# 44 Cast Parties

> Your self doesn't stop with your skin. It doesn't even stop with your history. You are everybody who lives, and everybody who ever lived; and the music you make eventually is the music of your humanity.
>
> – *Allaudin Mathieu*

*You said something earlier that really caught my ear; I think it was about cast parties. Can you tell me more about that?*

Ah yes, cast parties, one of our favorite subjects. It's a perspective not unlike the ancient Norse story of Summerland.

*The Norse? Let me guess… I would imagine they'd love the idea of a place where it's always summer, and there's plenty to eat, right?*

Absolutely, though perhaps more germane to our discussion is that Summerland, where the Norse believed they went when they died, was filled with family and friends who had survived to fight another day. Those lost in battle would be reunited with their comrades as well as their sworn enemies, and would then proceed to regale each other with tall tales of their extreme bravery and amazing fighting prowess. We have attended many thousands of cast parties, and they are indeed grand celebrations.

*Sounds like one hell of a celebration, all right, but I don't understand what that has to do with cast parties.*

We are simply using the general theme of Summerland as an introduction to our teaching about cast parties. Imagine that when you die you find yourself at a huge party in an exquisite, exotic setting, perhaps on a tropical beach, or in the high mountains, maybe in a majestic grove of giant redwoods. Then see yourself there with everyone you ever knew during your lifetime – parents, siblings, spouses, children, cousins, coaches, teachers and mentors; those who bullied you, or whom you bullied – *everyone.*

If you murdered someone (and no, we're not implying anything), they would be standing next to you, and vice versa. Farther out in the crowd, you may spot friends, family and lovers from other lifetimes. If you look carefully, you will realize that you know every single one of the many thousands of people at this party. Can you picture that scene?

*Yes, actually, I can. Vividly.*

Sweet. So here is what makes it a cast party. Everyone there is fully cognizant that they are all precious sparks of God, and that they had been playing their roles full out during the lifetime they had shared. There is no fear present, none at all. No resentment, no bitterness, no guilt, shame or anger. Just like the cast party at the end of any play, all the actors are well aware that they were playing a part. The funny thing is, the better an actor does in playing their part, the easier it is for the other actors to get into their roles as well, and everyone has a blast.

*You mean someone who had been viciously murdered would be high-five'n it with their murderer? That's messed-up!*

This is advanced material, to be sure. We are giving you a peek at a very high perspective, so please put what we are saying in that context. We do not in any way condone violence against another except in clear cases of self-preservation. Think of it this way: every murderer needs a victim, just as every day needs a night. Between incarnations, you make arrangements to take turns with various roles. In one life you may choose the experience of being murdered, in another you may very well take the part of a murderer, though of course it can (and often does) happen during a single incarnation.

*Why would anyone do that? Wait, I know, for the adrenaline rush! That must be it.*

That's certainly one component. It's quite similar to why an actor would choose to play the villain, the victim or the hero. None of these roles would have any meaning without the others. There is also the issue of acting out of your wounds, which we have already discussed at some length.

*You're not saying this is OK?*

We are not passing judgment; we're saying that this is the "isness" as it is currently experienced, not how it has to be. One of our core teachings is that you can make (and we would love to see all of humanity make) other choices. One of the reasons we wrote this book is to say in the strongest possible terms: you can create stories that are free of violence and still lead richly rewarding lives. But you cannot make any changes when you're convinced that you're helpless victims. Notice how making someone else responsible for doing it differently places power in their hands as well.

*I think I see where you're going here. This is another way of talking about the evolution of consciousness you mentioned earlier, isn't it?*

It is indeed. Before you can go somewhere else, it is essential to know where you are now. We are one of many voices speaking about how Consciousness itself may evolve. Remember, life is making all this up. There is the "isness." Then there are the stories that give the "isness" a context, or meaning. Duality no more requires violence than we require your belief in us for us to be. Violence is a choice masquerading as a necessity. Much like suffering, violence is optional.

*Violence is a choice masquerading as a necessity? I love it! But what if I forget and yell at someone, or get pissed when someone cuts me off on the freeway?*

Well, among other choices, including seeing such events as gifts, they can be viewed as AFOGs.

*Excuse me? AFOGs?*

Another Fabulous Opportunity For Growth. It's another, perhaps more humorous, way to see every experience of life as a gift. Just in case you've forgotten, or no one ever told you, laughter really is the best medicine. Not laughter *at*, laughter *with*. The joke is not on you, the joke *is* you. You are the comedian, the joke, the punch line, the stage *and* the audience. As Jackson Browne sings on his song *The Pretender*, "We can be a happy idiot, struggling for the legal tender," or you can wake up and sing another song, yet to be written. In each moment, you have a new opportunity to choose.

*That's easy to say when you're not mourning the death of a loved one. Sometimes life just isn't funny, at least not to me.*

Of course not. Sometimes the only thing to do is howl in agony. Laughter, tears, it's all part of this dance of duality. As we have seen, feelings, when felt fully, inevitably shift. However, at cast parties there is mostly laughter. If there are tears, they are tears of relief, of release, of recognition and of joy.

*Yeah, I can only imagine. I guess that a sure sign of whether we're taking ourselves too seriously would be a shortage of laughter in our lives.*

Exactly. We're giving you this perspective on cast parties to help remind you that God-As-Us is all there is, passionately staging this magnificent miracle called life. The next time you see a friend, family member, anyone at all – perhaps the clerk checking you out at the store, that person cutting you off on the freeway, your mother-in-law – just remember that they are God, and treat them accordingly. We're confident that doing so will transform your life.

# 45 Gaia

> You may find it hard to swallow the notion that anything as large and apparently inanimate as the Earth is alive. Surely, you may say, the Earth is almost wholly rock, and nearly all incandescent with heat. The difficulty can be lessened if you let the image of a giant redwood tree enter your mind. The tree undoubtedly is alive, yet 99% of it is dead. The great tree is an ancient spire of dead wood, made of lignin and cellulose by the ancestors of the thin layer of living cells which constitute its bark. How like the Earth, and more so when we realize that many of the atoms of the rocks far down into the magma were once part of the ancestral life of which we all have come.
>
> – *James Lovelock*

*We've spent a lot of time talking about personal healing, but I have the distinct impression that you have much more to share.*

Given OurSelf away, have we? Actually, we have several books worth of material still to share. There comes a time, though, for every journey to end, and so it is with *Drunk with Wonder*. Unless you have something in particular you want us to touch on, we will go ahead and see about tying our book into a tidy little knot before we bid you a fond adios.

*But there's so much more I want to talk about! Let's see...how about the environment? You've described the world as being a stage for our Great Passion Play, but is it more than a stage with great props and scenery?*

More? Of course, there is much, much more! From our perspective, "more" hardly seems adequate to describe the infinite possibilities of the multiverse. However, you asked specifically about whether the environment is more than a stage. Since we've seen that God is all there is, Mother Earth is God too, just as you are. This planet you are graced to live on is far more than a simple stage.

Over the millennia, many have known this world as Gaia, your Earth Mother. The winds form Her breath, the rivers Her veins, the ocean currents Her arteries, the forests Her lungs, and the estuaries Her kidneys. Molten fire, an echo of Father sun, glows at Her core. All life on Earth is an extension of Gaia, birthed out of the fiery furnace of Gaia's vast heart.

*Excuse me? Didn't you say life was an expression of God, that God's gift of love was life itself?*

Good memory. And that is so. If you'll bear with us, we're asking you to consider a vastly larger perspective. Begin with sub-atomic particles which, as we have seen, constantly wink in and out of the universe. Elements, such as hydrogen, oxygen, carbon, iron and all the rest, indeed every single atom composing your solar system, the galaxy and much, much more, were all forged in the immense furnaces of stars that have already lived and died, seeding the universe through titanic explosions known as supernovas. You are, quite literally, star seed.

As many scientists have noted, particularly James Lovelock, whose 1979 book, *Gaia: A New Look at Life on Earth*, has turned out to be quite prescient, the laws of physics, as applied to this planet, have made life inevitable. And we assure you that life is by no means limited to this planet. That whole notion is so stunningly anthropocentric!

Anyhow, back to the environment. For at least the past couple of billion years, Gaia has been regulating Herself in a way that eventually encouraged you to show up. This exquisite regulatory mechanism uses rivers, forests, plankton, ice caps, everything, as essential components of this planetary organism.

*So that's why things seem so out of whack with the weather these days, because we've been damming rivers and cutting down forests? It sounds as though we've really been screwing around with Gaia.*

And, if you have been paying attention, you will have noticed that Gaia has been screwing back. Though there are much larger forces at play, global warming is no myth. Don't think for a moment that hurricane Katrina and other so-called "natural" disasters have no human component.

For example, much of the loss of life can be traced back to decisions made (or not made) to ride out the storm, or even to move into those vulnerable coastal areas in the first place. From our perspective, though, humans are not remotely as powerful a force on Gaia as some would have you believe. The worst you could do would be to make the planet uninhabitable for yourselves. Gaia will not die. Life will continue.

*I guess that's good news. For life, I mean. You don't sound all that hopeful for human beings.*

Dear one, if we had no hope we wouldn't be speaking with you now. You see, humans are as much a part of Gaia as the wind and the mountains. Not more, but not less either. We ask you to step into this majestic "long view" perspective we have been speaking of. We are suggesting that humans also hold crucial roles as part of Gaia. You are Her compassionate heart, and also the functional equivalent of Her cerebral cortex, or thinking brain. Moreover, through the Internet, you are wiring yourselves up as a much more integrated brain. For the first time in the history of your species, you are making your accumulated knowledge and wisdom available to anyone, anywhere with access to the Internet.

*That's easier said than done, especially in developing countries.*

True enough. But did you know that dedicated humanitarians are developing technology that allows for incredibly inexpensive, wireless access, including hardware that is simple, rugged and easy to manufacture and repair? Portable Fabrication Shops (FABs)[36] small enough to fit in a garage are just the beginning.

*I must say that your perspective is fascinating, and certainly more hopeful than I first imagined. But when I look around the world, I see people starving while others die from chronic overeating. I see an oil crisis, fanatic terrorism, and in general more and more people competing for fewer and fewer resources. What do you have to say about all of that?*

For us to address these questions fully would take more time than we have in this book. For now, please understand that these are resource issues that are eminently solvable with your boundless creativity, compassionate hearts and planetary resolve. On a planetary scale you grow plenty of food, and there are still huge stocks of hydrocarbons left to be exploited, if you so choose. Of course, if you do chose to continue burning hydrocarbons, unhappy consequences will multiply like weeds.

As we discussed earlier, you are still living under a meta-story that dominates your world. We call it FBC. It is out of this deep, fear-based root that the whole notion of scarcity arises. In this case, we're speaking of a perceived scarcity of food and fuel, resources which are seen as things to be acquired and exploited as cheaply as possible, then resold at the highest profit.

Paul Hawken, Amory Lovins, and L. Hunter Lovins, in their brilliant book, *Natural Capitalism*, argue that since the entire planet is our collective home (Buckminster Fuller coined the term *Spaceship Earth*), people need to acknowledge the enormous value of the resources that they are currently stripping out of Mother Gaia. Hydrocarbons are not a renewable resource, at least not in any meaningful sense of the term, and when they're burned, they contribute mightily to toxic pollution and global warming. While inherently there is no lack of energy available, there has been a lack of planetary will to switch to renewable, non-polluting sources of energy.

Yes, today people are quite needlessly starving. They are also dying of pollution, AIDS, malaria and savage violence. None of it is preordained. There is no question as to what must be done, and many healthy ways to accomplish these goals. You need only the will.

*I get it! How we care for our environment is not only a reflection of how we treat each other, but how much we appreciate this amazing web of life we're a part of.*

That's it exactly. When you thoughtlessly discard trash out the window, foul your air, water and earth, it's just like messing yourselves.

*But only a crazy person, or an idiot, would do that!*

Or a baby. Remember, we're suggesting that Gaia is growing a cerebral cortex, with each human the rough equivalent of a brain cell. It takes time and loving patience to teach a baby not to mess itself. That's where you are as a species, just at the toddler stage, beginning to learn about a larger world. You have the power to stop plundering and destroying your Home while still enjoying lives filled with peace and extraordinary abundance.

*I love the way you think! But let's say we do succeed in wiring up this planetary brain, and we do figure out how to manifest abundance for everyone. Then what?*

Whatever you choose to create. For many of you, living your lives in love will be enough. Peacefully enjoying the miracle of life with family and friends, making a difference in the world, can truly be the life of your dreams. For those who want more, you're still evolving, right? How about the evolution of consciousness itself? Imagine Gaia-As-Us, an awakened planet, making contact with other awakened planets, creating connections in ways you cannot begin to imagine, wiring up a Galactic mind.

*Now you've done it. My mind just got blown to smithereens. I don't think I'm quite ready for that huge a perspective. Um, perhaps we could spend a moment on something you just mentioned about the evolution of consciousness. I thought that conscious awareness was the changeless "isness" of God-As-Us. How could that evolve?*

## Seed of my Body

I'm becoming transparent to my past
Like a ghost freed from Karmic chains

I float above my Earthly form
Taking refuge in the Sacred,

Forged from Gaia
Seed of my own body

Chiseled mountain air flowing
Relentlessly through my hair

Orange hearth-fire glowing
Through molten eyes

Snowmelt streaming conversationally
Along awakening streambeds

Spirit spark cadencing my heart
Wings straining against dying light

Weaving love through
Seven generations

Flowering Stardancers
Seed of the One –

# 46 Evolution of Consciousness

Truth is not gender-based.
– *Mike Colgan*

As we've discussed, you are playing the ultimate game of hide and seek. A posse (or perhaps passel) of God chose to manifest as this universe, and in so doing set up the Great Passion Play. This play has evolved over time, to the moment you find yourselves inhabiting right here and right now.

The entire history of life on this planet is a story of God-As-Us hiding from YourSelf so you can shout "Boo!" to each other. You explore just how far you can go feeling separate and alone, only to eventually, and quite inevitably, call the game on account of consciousness.

*So, if I understand you, when everyone wakes up to the truth of who we really are, the Great Passion Play is over?*

The version that appears to be run by FBC does indeed draw to a close, to thunderous applause. However, that in no way means that humans, or life in general, would suddenly vanish, or Ascend, or whatever. Life continues. Remember, in an infinite universe there are endless possibilities and permutations to explore. You can have all the fun and excitement of life without so much fear and suffering. It's your choice.

*Sounds fabulous, but I'm still struggling with the idea of consciousness evolving. What does it evolve into?*

Greater and greater awareness. In the last chapter, we spoke of the Gaia mind wiring up, and in your perhaps not-so-distant future connecting to a Galactic Mind. Conscious awareness evolves out of self-awareness, sourcing its experience rather than imagining itself to be a victim. There is still a sense of self and other, all the way up to one Galactic Mind connecting with another.

Much closer to your home world, the evolution of consciousness refers to the truth that as people Awaken, they make it easier for the next generation to Awaken. Imagine it as a snowball, gathering speed as it gains mass. Simply put, Awakening no longer requires decades of dedicated meditation. The tools we have shared in this book will, if faithfully applied, get you started on your way.

*If I'm understanding you, we could see the entire life cycle of the universe, from the big bang to planetary awakening and beyond, as God creating a vast playground in which to play the game of hide and seek you keep mentioning. All these sparks of God start out feeling lost and alone, filled with fear, and over the ages of the universe gradually reconnect every spark until, at the end, there is once again only One of us here.*

Well said, dear one! Quite succinctly put. The evolution of consciousness is the spiritual equivalent of life evolving from single cells to your present circumstances. Eons ago, your bodies began by connecting disparate, separate cells into larger, more sophisticated structures. Though humans have only been around for a few hundred thousand years, distant ancestors had developed a bipedal structure, with eyes, ears, a mouth and so forth several hundred million years ago.

Now, with these bodies, these hands, hearts, minds and spirits, you are already well along towards creating heaven right here on Gaia. In fact, from an Enlightened perspective, you already have. For many thousands of years, awakening to the God within took incredible dedication and immense courage, and was an extremely rare phenomenon.

Wisdom teachings from Awakened Masters, including Buddha, Jesus, Mohammad, Ramana Maharshi and others, still strongly resonate with many today.

As each Awakening occurs, increased wisdom and awareness ripple out into the pool of planetary consciousness, making it a bit less onerous for the next Awakening. And so it goes. What was once available only to the initiate who had spent a lifetime in solitary reflection is now far more accessible.

Of course, from our perspective, awakening to the God within is only the first step. The Awakened state allows you to live your lives in love, but it does not, in and of itself, get the laundry done. This subject is thoroughly discussed in Jack Kornfield's excellent book, *After the Ecstasy, the Laundry*.

The essence of this perennial wisdom is simply that ecstatic states of profound spiritual bliss, where you float serenely in the ocean of joy, is your birthright. Staying in this state of blissful awareness can even seem effortless, particularly during meditation within a spiritual community or in deep communion with nature. The trick is learning to maintain this peaceful state of loving-kindness while doing the laundry, the dishes, perhaps taking out the trash. The truth is that God manifests in the seemingly mundane as much as anywhere.

*I think I understand. It's like being on vacation from the routine, when it's often much easier to be in a good mood and enjoying life. It's when life becomes challenging that the ocean of joy seems furthest away.*

Yes, that's the idea. Awakening into Conscious Awareness is an absolutely crucial step. Staying Awake through all the drama, apparent chaos and casual brutality in the world is quite another. While opening to states of Bliss is enormously valuable, learning to *stay* Awake no matter what is the game of mastery. You see, each moment presents you with another opportunity to choose love or fear. Choosing love makes it more available to everyone, everywhere. Choosing fear… well, we're well acquainted with where that leads, aren't we?

*Only too well acquainted, actually. I'm seeing FBC, which seemed to be so all-encompassing until recently, as just one choice. When we're able to see fear as a choice, we're able to see that there are other choices available, particularly love. And as more and more of us choose love, we become part of the transformation of our entire world.*

Yes, that is indeed when transformation becomes possible. Your Awakening inevitably leads to seeking out others who understand. Communities coalesce around wisdom teachings much as flowers bloom around up-welling springs. Once healthy communities become established, they begin to connect with one another. Using a combination of tools, many of which we have discussed in this book, you can explore questions such as, "What legacy do you wish to pass on to your children, your grandchildren and on to generations yet unborn?"

*You mean tools such as the breathing meditation, healthy expression of emotions, dropping the waterline and getting real, conscious language, and remembering to choose love over fear?*

You got it. The entire planet could choose to Awaken 'in the twinkling of an eye," and you'd still have countless adventures to share, complete with mountains of adrenaline for all. Nursing your forests, rivers, air and oceans back to health; putting an end to disease, war, hunger and separation; in short, creating a world where everyone wins; it's all well within your grasp. Not only that, you can create all that your hearts desire while, in the process, having more fun than you would ever have imagined possible.

*But what about aging, accidents and death? Surely you're not suggesting we can eliminate those?*

Eliminate? No. What you can eliminate, though, is being so afraid of them. Accidents will happen. Tsunamis, earthquakes, hurricanes, mudslides, volcanic eruptions, and wildfires are all part of life.

Remember our discussion about duality. Aging makes your youth just that much more precious. The possibility that you, or those you're closest to, could be off the planet in a heartbeat invites you into an ever-deepening appreciation for each miraculous moment you have to share with one another.

We say again: part of Awakening is the profound realization that it's all perfect just the way it is, while at the same moment passionately choosing love and service. The deepest joy you can know is that which comes when you allow your broken-open hearts to pour forth the limitless, sublime, ever available nectar of loving-kindness. Truly, as Don Henley sings on "Everything is Different Now," from his superb album *Inside Job*, "We get the love that we allow."

# 47 Broken Open

A person who can see nothing but God everywhere has lost the ability to either hurt or be hurt. By virtue of being completely and totally defenseless, they become invincible.

– *Deepak Chopra*

*Our hearts have to break? You mean like falling in love and it not working out? I hate that part!*

We're intimately familiar with love in its many forms, so we deeply appreciate just how painful love can feel. However, your hearts don't "have" to break. In truth, there is not a single spark of God anywhere who is not what we would call a volunteer.

*Why on God's Green Earth would anyone volunteer to go through the experience of falling in love, only to go through the burning agony of being spurned? What good could come of that?*

Ah, dear one, we feel you. You could only ask that from the perspective of having been there and felt the sting. Your hearts do indeed feel as though they're breaking when someone you love a lot is no longer there for you. Perhaps your mother dies, or a spouse. One of the saddest experiences of all can be the loss of a child.

*My God, I can't even imagine something so terrible. How could a person even go on living?*

It's not an easy thing, to say the least. There is no more certain way to feel your heart ripped completely out of your chest than to deal with losing a child, a spouse, any close family member or even a friend. For many, even losing a treasured pet can engender similar feelings.

Whenever your life force dances with another in an intimate, loving way, you literally take on some of the other's essence. When you are fully present to this process, it is one of the most sublime opportunities for ecstasy God-As-Us has ever manifested. It is also a great way to guarantee that your species will continue.

Yet, as we have seen repeatedly in the dance of duality, to love full out means risking it all. There is nothing quite like the adrenaline rush of adoring your child, and nothing quite like the overwhelming agony of losing that child, whether to war, starvation, disease, violence, suicide or an accident

*I just don't think I could ever have a child, especially with the way things are in this crazy world.*

You always, of course, have a choice. No one is keeping score, judging that life must be lived a certain way *or else*. Perhaps the very greatest act of courage is the choice to have children in the first place. In general, opening one's heart to another contains risk. At any time, when you least expect it, they can be gone. Every day, parents bury children, lovers bury their beloveds, and friends mourn the loss of friends.

This price is what you pay for making friends, falling (or better yet, *rising*) in love, or bringing children into the world. That is the way of it, the flip side of the coin of life, of your dance with duality. In the "isness" of life, things, people and experiences come and go. Remember, dear one, it is not the "isness," it's how you are with it, which determines whether you spend your life in fear or celebration. It is the difference between broken hearts and hearts broken open.

*I still don't understand the difference. Broken is broken, isn't it?*

We can appreciate that, to one whose heart feels broken, the distinction can seem meaningless. However, part of our teaching is that there is, in actuality, an enormous difference. Think of it this way: a broken heart is one that has shattered, like glass. Hearts that are rigid, held tight in the grip of fear, break all too easily when outer conditions don't meet their expectations.

Hearts can shatter whenever someone believes that their needs, including their need for love, must be met by someone else, whether from a parent, spouse, child or friend. If there is a divorce, a falling-out or a death, their victim-consciousness cranks into high gear. Their love has been conditional, brittle, the breath perpetually held. It is love with a grasping, closed fist.

On the other hand, a heart that breaks open cannot shatter. While it breaks for sure, again and again, it continues sourcing love. This unconditional love cascades through the opening as a torrent of snowmelt floods down a mountain in springtime, continually giving to others as unconditionally as the sun gives to Gaia.

A child who comes through you is not yours. They do not come here to "make" you happy, or even, as many parents of teenagers may think, to test your limits and make you crazy at every opportunity. They come to share the miracle of life. That sharing may last only for a heartbeat, though you hope it will last a lifetime. The heart's deepest treasure is the quality of the shared connection, rather than the quantity.

*Whoa, that's intense. It never occurred to me to look at it that way before. I certainly agree that parents are crazy brave. When I think about it, I realize that the vast majority of parents do get to see their children grow up and have children of their own. That's comforting.*

Bringing life through you in such an awesomely intimate way is the great gamble, and in so doing becomes the greatest gift you can bestow. As you have seen with your primal emotions, your survival instincts run very deep. We've spoken a bit about procreation, but it by no means stops there. You also have profound nurturing instincts. To come between parent and child is to come to a whole new appreciation of "fierce protector."

There is no doubt that losing a child is an over-the-top, life-changing experience. A strong heart will break wide open; a fragile heart will surely shatter. The compassionate heart breaks open for all concerned. A resilient heart, a healthy heart, can break open, allowing torrents of intense emotions to be fully felt, instead of stuffing one's balloon to the bursting point.

*That actually makes sense. Though a parent might feel overwhelming pain if they were to lose a child, they wouldn't be creating suffering on top of the pain if they were willing to allow their feelings to wash over them.*

Well put. And we wish to point out that it is one thing to have a conversation about this issue, and quite another to go through such an experience. We have known parents who, out of their own agony, found the strength to start a support group for others who had lost a child. Other parents, with no awareness of a larger perspective, shatter, and can never put their hearts, or lives, back together again. We invoke oceans of compassion for all those lost in this or any other experience of suffering.

# 48 Faith

Faith is an oasis in the heart, which will never
be reached by the caravan of thinking.
– *Kahlil Gibran*

*I guess it all comes down to faith.*

Pardon?

*Well, we've talked a lot about God-As-Us creating this Great Passion Play I'm living in. You've painted quite a glorious picture of why I'm here and what a miracle it all is. I think I finally understand how my beliefs and stories shape my experience, and I believe that I'll never again look at death with as much fear as I used to.*

*But at the end of the day, there's no overt, obvious, incontrovertible proof that your perspective has any more merit than another's. Spiritual beliefs are just that, beliefs. So ultimately, as I said, it's about faith. After all, faith means, "Belief that is not based on proof."*

Of course. As we have said from the beginning, we are simply presenting another perspective, another story. Not *the* perspective, *a* perspective. Not *the* story, *a* story. If you find it useful, and it sounds as though, from what you just said, that you do, then we are grateful to have been given the opportunity to make a contribution. What you do with this perspective is up to you. We have pointed out a few of the multitude of ways that exist to make your own contribution, should you be so moved.

*But it still seems as though we need faith in order to imagine a hopeful future, especially with the way things are in the world.*

Really? Even after all the positive things we've talked about? We guarantee that for every negative event you care to focus on, we can point out at least two others that are positive. Remember, it's not the "isness…."

*Yeah, I know, it's how we are with the "isness." I get it, I really do. It just seems as though we're making choices more on faith than anything else.*

Actually, you're making choices based specifically on the stories and beliefs you choose to tell yourself. The only thing that has changed is that you're becoming conscious that you have choices about which stories you're listening to. What we are asking you to do is spend some time with this new perspective. One possibility would be to keep a journal for 30 days, writing down every time you notice that you are at a choice-point. Include the choice you made as well as some of those you didn't make. Also, keep track of all the things, events and people for which you feel grateful.

I promise you, if you do this faithfully for a solid month, your life will be transformed. Yes, dear one, we are well aware that we used the word "faithfully." In this case, consider using the meaning: "Confidence or trust in a person or thing." Of course you will embark on this adventure "on faith." If you already knew for a fact that this approach to life would work for you, no faith would be required. Think about it. What do you have to lose except your fear-based way of looking at the world?

*Hmmm… OK, I see your point. I guess I just did it again, didn't I?*

You mean changed your focus from LBC to FBC?

*That would be it.*

You're doing an excellent job of noticing how easily the mind can shift from one to the other. So, remember what you've learned about breathing. As soon as you notice fear, simply breathe into it until excitement floods your cells. Be sure to look for the gift in the experience. And remember Quan Yin. Any time you become aware that you're lost in FBC, call in mercy, compassion and forgiveness.

How about this: as we have suggested, take the next 30 days to thoroughly explore the ideas and perspectives we have shared in this book. We say again, keep a journal, feel your feelings, choose love. Just let go of your fear, misery and doubt for 30 days. If at the end of that time you're absolutely convinced it's all a crock, we'll happily refund your misery. We'll even refund what you paid for this book. (Please be sure to keep a receipt, and only one refund per household.)

*Wow, that's quite an offer. You certainly seem to have faith in all this.*

Well, if you're suggesting that we have faith, we humbly disagree. We *live* in the Ocean of Joy, remember? We don't need faith to live there, any more than you need faith to read this book. Now, if you're saying we have faith in you, of course we do. Your whole life can be viewed in the context of faith lost and found. Perhaps some of you reading this book will dismiss our perspective as the delusional ranting of a fool.

We trust utterly that those who will find our teachings and perspective useful will find themselves drawn to our work, while others will not be at all. You see, either LBC works for you, or it doesn't. We are not here to judge you, whatever your choice. We choose love. We invite you to choose love as well, and join with us in creating a world where love wins.

*So you think that this perspective you've been sharing will continue to work for me?*

Absolutely, as long as you apply these principles and jump off the cliff of your fears. Keep trusting your own heart. We promise you will be rewarded beyond your wildest dreams.

*OK, as long as we're clear that you're asking me to jump on faith.*

As long as you jump. We feel that we have provided ample evidence for our perspective. We have seen that faith is equated with trust, just as we've seen that there can be no deep and abiding love without trust. We're advocating that you trust enough to jump off the cliff of your fears, and that you will be caught in the arms of love. Until you directly experience *how* making different choices creates different results, having some faith will prove to be eminently useful. Have enough faith in love, and in yourself, to stay safe when you jump. What we can tell you is that, from our perspective, it's worth it. All you really have to lose is your fear.

*You're right, I'm stalling. Promise you'll be there for me?*

Always, dear one. But more importantly, *you'll* always be there for you. You are not separate and alone. We are One....

# 49 Journey's End

Your full heart radiating outward is the greatest gift and the most important contribution you can make to our aching world.

– *Debbie Ford*

And so, dear one, we find ourselves at the end of our journey together. It is such an honor to travel along this path of awakening with you. We have touched on many subjects, given you much to contemplate and, we trust, had some fun along the way.

*I must admit I'm feeling some sadness. I really, really don't want this to end, or for you to leave!*

Where would we go? There is only right here, right now. Whenever you notice you're stuck in fear (and it may help to think of fear as False Evidence Appearing Real), just breathe. Fear is excitement without breath, and breathing unlocks your authentic power. It's your life. How will you live now that you know you have choices?

*It seems so clear to me how my beliefs and stories create my experience. I'm sure I'll be grokking the implications and repercussions of that for the rest of my life.*

No doubt. We urge you not to become too attached to any of your beliefs, as seeing the world through fresh eyes is an essential component of the Awakened Heart. As John Lilly said in his book *Center of the Cyclone*, "Beliefs are limits." If we wish to grow and expand into a larger, more comprehensive perspective, we must be continually willing to let go of beliefs that no longer serve us, and then be willing to take on those that do.

*You mean there is always a larger perspective available, forever?*

For all practical purposes, especially in the context of your human life, yes. But part of the paradox of duality is that one can hold the certainty of belief *at the same moment* that one also groks the infinite nature of Being.

Awakening to the God within is a journey, not a destination. Having said that, we ask you this question: Would you rather be a seeker or a finder?

*Um, is that a trick question? How can I find anything unless I seek?*

Well, you could stumble across some truth and be present enough to recognize its value. But there's a deeper point here. You see, when you identify with being a seeker, you will forever be looking for answers. If you were actually to find that which you were seeking, your very identity as a seeker could be threatened. So, no matter what truths you may uncover, as long as you remain invested in your identity as a seeker, they can never be enough. So you continue seeking, as in, "I seek, therefore I am."

A finder, on the other hand, lives from the perspective that one can indeed find perennial wisdom. This wisdom then serves as a touchstone, allowing the finder to direct the vast love pouring through their broken-open hearts out into the world in some form of service, or seva. Selfless service is one of the most certain signs of an awakened heart.

*So it sounds as though one of the surest signs of Awakening is to actually engage in the world in a way that supports the free flowing of LBC.*

We could not have put it more succinctly. Remember, you can't do life wrong, only with more or less suffering, and more or less awareness. Life is not about a specific action or activity, it's about how much love you can infuse it with. Every time you choose love, you make more love available to the whole world. And then there is the next moment, and with it a fresh opportunity.

*In this moment, I choose love. I also choose to thank you for your kindness, patience, and most of all your good-humored love. I have no doubt that participating in this book has already changed my life. I can feel it in my heart, which seems about to burst.*

Dear one, you are entirely welcome. It is our seva, or service, and we are grateful for the opportunity.

Namaste.

> When we come to it
> We must confess that we are the possible
> We are the miraculous, the true wonder of this
> world
> That is when, and only when
> We come to it
>
> – *Maya Angelou*

# Oneness

If Oneness is the ocean,
And we but waves rolling free,
Then what we call our identity
Simply comes and goes,
Ever flowing
Onto the beach
Of our consciousness,

Rising like the sun to
Look out in wonder
On manifest creation before
Sinking back in Bliss,
Reabsorbed into the One

We play,
As children,
Where the waves
Meet the shore

We build castles
Made of sand
Watch them wash
Back out to sea
All things manifest
From this thin strand
We let go of our knowing
And simply Be –

# Notes

**Introduction**

1. www.hypnotherapycenter.com.

**Chapter 1**

2. For a more thorough grounding in M-theory, see: http://www.damtp.cam.ac.uk/user/gr/public/qg_ss.html.

3. For a thorough discussion of the Twin Slit Experiment, see http://www.hotquanta.com/twinslit.html.

**Chapter 7**

4. By bringing body, mind, and breath into oneness through the practice of sitting meditation, the practitioner is able to become concentrated, to look deeply, to understand, and to love. Drawing upon Mahayana texts such as *The Heart Sutra* and the *Diamond That Cuts Through Illusion Sutra*, the practitioner comes to understand "inter-being" with all life, and acts appropriately. Throughout, emphasis is placed not only on formal sitting and walking meditation, but also upon how to incorporate basic Buddhist mindfulness practice into our daily activities. See Thich Nhat Hanh in the bibliography.

**Chapter 8**

5. If you choose to record this exercise, please allow at least five minutes before continuing with the next statement.

**Chapter 9**

6. Beyondananda, Swami. *Driving Your Own Karma*. Rochester: Destiny Books, 1989.

7. See chapter 11.

**Chapter 10**

8. Grok: To understand profoundly through intuition or empathy. Originally coined by Robert A. Heinlein in his book *Stranger in a Strange Land*.

**Chapter 11**

9. Wolf, Fred Alan. *Parallel Universes*. New York: Touchstone, 1988.

10. Kotler, Steven. "Extreme States." *Discover Magazine*, July 2005.

11. See www.masterysystems.com for much more on the use of conscious language.

12. For more about the teachings of Science of Mind, see http://www.rsintl.org/.

**Chapter 12**

13. Baker, Stephen and Aston, Adam. "The Business of Nanotech." Businessweek Online, Feb. 14, 2005.

14. For a thorough discussion of the Twin Slit Experiment, see http://www.hotquanta.com/twinslit.html.

15. The "Butterfly Effect," or more technically the "sensitive dependence on initial conditions", is the essence of chaos. Chaos theory, in mathematics and physics, deals with the behavior of certain nonlinear dynamical systems that (under certain conditions) exhibit the phenomenon known as chaos, most famously characterized by

sensitivity to initial conditions. Examples of such systems include the atmosphere, the solar system, plate tectonics, turbulent fluids, economies, and population growth.

Systems that exhibit mathematical chaos are deterministic and thus orderly in some sense; this technical use of the word chaos is at odds with common parlance, which suggests complete disorder. When we say that chaos theory studies deterministic systems, it is necessary to mention a related field of physics called quantum chaos theory that studies non-deterministic systems following the laws of quantum mechanics. Source: http://en.wikipedia.org/wiki/Chaos_theory.

16. See: Bub, Jeffrey, "Quantum Entanglement and Information," *The Stanford Encyclopedia of Philosophy (Winter 2002 Edition)*, Edward N. Zalta (ed.), URL = http://plato.stanford.edu/archives/win2002/entries/qt-entangle/. This discussion shows quite clearly that, at least at the quantum level, information can be exchanged in a non-local, simultaneous manner. We provide this discussion as further evidence that, in essence, not only are we all connected, we are One.

**Chapter 13**

17. Reference: http://www.personal.psu.edu/users/b/j/bjs286/astro/whatis.html.

The "Many Worlds Theory" was published in 1957 by Dr. Hugh Everett, III.

"In response to a number of troubling problems in quantum theory, particularly the problem of Schrodinger's Cat. Dr. Everett discovered a single concept that provided an adequate solution to many of the quantum paradoxes. The theory contests that for each possible outcome in any situation, the world splits into multiple worlds, or universes. A different "world" then exists for each of the possible outcomes. In each of these worlds, everything appears to be the same except for the result of the one choice that was made. Each of these worlds then branches off into its own future, and there is no way for these different universes to interact with one another.

"For example, imagine yourself at a friend's house several blocks away from your own home. Suppose your friend has seen too much of you today and asks you to leave immediately. You are now faced with a decision. You could walk home, drive your car, borrow your ungrateful friend's bike and ride home (fast), etc. There are multiple possible ways for you to accomplish the task of getting home. According to Many Worlds, *every one* of these possibilities actually happens. In one "world" you are walking home, in another you are starting your car and driving down the road. Reality has split into an infinite amount of worlds, as it does for every decision you make.

"This theory is certainly much more complicated from a scientific standpoint, but we will set aside wave collapsing and other complicated details for the sake of simplicity. To read more about the gritty details, consult the resources page. The Many Worlds theory has been accepted by many prominent scientists today including such names as Steven Hawking, Murray Gell-Mann, Steven Weinberg, and Richard Feynmann."

18. Tolle, Eckhart. *The Power of Now*. Novato: New World Library, 1999.

**Chapter 14**
19. Institute of Noetic Sciences (IONS): http://www.ions.org/.

20. Ardagh, Arjuna Nick. *Relaxing into Clear Seeing*. Grass Valley: Self X Press, 1998.

**Chapter 19**
21. Quinn, Daniel. *Ishmael*. New York: Bantam Books, 1995.

22. We recommend these books by Debbie Ford, *The Secret of the Shadow* and *Owning your Whole Story*, for a deeper understanding of these issues.

**Chapter 24**

23. www.medicineatmichigan.org/magazine/2001/fall/brain/default.asp.

24. Rodegast, Pat and Stanton, Judith. *Emmanuel's Book: A Manual for Living Comfortably in the Cosmos*. New York: Bantam Books, 1985.

**Chapter 27**

25. www.dictionary.com.

26. AC/DC.

27. Reich, Wilheim. *The Mass Psychology of Fascism*. New York: Farrar, Strauss & Giroux, 1980.

**Chapter 31**

28. Challenge Day, 2520 Stanwell Drive, Suite 160, Concord, CA 94520 – 925.957.0234 – www.challengeday.org.

**Chapter 33**

29. *What is Enlightment Magazine*, #17, Spring/Summer 2000. www.wie.org/j17/self_acceptance.asp?ifr=dp&ifd=17.

30. *What the Bleep Do We Know!?* dir. Mark Vicente, Betsy Chasse & William Arntz. Captured Light Industries presents A Lord of the Wind Film, 2004, video recording. www.whatthebleep.com.

**Chapter 36**

31. Kurtz, Rod. "Innovations: Prophylactic Yuks," Businessweek, March 21, 2005.

**Chapter 37**
32. Czimbal, Bob and Zadikov, Maggie. *A Guide to Healthy Touch: Vitamin T*. Australia: Open Book Pub., 1991.

**Chapter 39**
33. Historian Lord Acton (1834-1902) in a letter to Bishop Mandell Creighton, 1887.

**Chapter 43**
34. Stewart, Katrine. *A Book of Life: Spiritual Journaling in the Twenty-First Century*. Bolivar: Quiet Waters Publications, 2000.

35. We highly recommend the following people and organizations for in-depth personal work:

- Challenge Day (www.challengeday.org.)
- Debbie Ford (Ford Institute for Integrative Coaching) http://www.debbieford.com/)
- Human Awareness Institute (http://www.hai.org/)
- The Landmark Forum (http://www.landmarkeducation.com/)

**Chapter 45**
36. Gershenfeld, Neil. *FAB: The Coming Revolution on Your Desktop – From Personal Computers to Personal Fabricators*. New York: Basic Books, 2005.

# Glossary

**Acclimate:** To accustom or become accustomed to a new environment or situation; adapt.

**AFOG:** Another Fabulous Opportunity for Growth. Any event or experience in our lives that we notice as having value in helping us create the world of our dreams.

**Amrita:** The ambrosia, prepared by the Hindu gods, that bestows immortality.

**Anthropocentric:** Regarding humans as the central element of the universe.

**Discernment:** The act or process of exhibiting keen insight and good judgment.

**Disparagement:** A communication that belittles somebody or something.

**Dropping the Waterline:** Used to signify the act of letting go of our stories and getting real.

**Ego:** A unique collection of stories constructed of thoughts, feelings and beliefs around which coalesces the pearl of the personality.

**Empirical:** Verifiable or provable by means of observation or experiment.

**Fear-Based-Consciousness (FBC)**: The dominant paradigm in our culture. Through this perspective, life is seen as "hard," and other people as "out to get you." When we see through eyes of fear, everything and everyone is a threat.

**fMRI**: functional Magnetic Resonance Imaging. This state-of-the-art technology allows researchers to "see" the brain functioning in real time.

**Grok (grokking, grokked)**: [from the novel "Stranger in a Strange Land", by Robert A. Heinlein, where it is a Martian word meaning literally `to drink' and metaphorically `to be one with'] The emphatic form is `grok in fullness'. It means to understand, usually in a global sense. Connotes intimate, infinitive and exhaustive knowledge.

**Inextricably**: Difficult or impossible to disentangle or untie.

**Intrinsically**: Of or relating to the essential nature of a thing; inherent.

**Insidious**: Working or spreading harmfully in a subtle or stealthy manner.

**Isness**: The way things are, devoid of our (often fear-based) stories of how things should (or should not) be.

**Intuition:** The act or faculty of knowing or sensing without the use of rational processes; immediate cognition.

**Jones:** An addiction, especially to heroin.

**Lifestream**: 1. An entire life span from birth to death. 2. The force, or energy, that animates matter.

**Love-Based-Consciousness (LBC):** A paradigm in which the entire multiverse is held as Sacred and Holy. Through this perspective, life is seen as a gift, and other people as infinitely precious sparks of God.

**Multiverse:** (or meta-universe) is the hypothetical set of multiple possible universes, including the observable universe, which comprise the whole of physical reality.

**Ostentatious:** Intended to attract notice and impress others.

**Panoply:** A complete and impressive array.

**Paradigm:** A set of assumptions, concepts, values, and practices that constitutes a way of viewing reality for the community that shares them, especially in an intellectual discipline.

**Plethora:** Extreme excess or fullness.

**Prescient:** Perceiving the significance of events before they occur.

**Reductionism (reductionist):** An attempt or tendency to explain a complex set of facts, entities, phenomena, or structures by another, simpler set: "For the last 400 years science has advanced by reductionism... The idea is that you could understand the world, all of nature, by examining smaller and smaller pieces of it. When assembled, the small pieces would explain the whole" (John Holland).

**Reprehensible:** Bringing or deserving severe rebuke or censure.

**Scarcity Consciousness:** The idea that there is only so much of something, such as love, to go around, and for anyone to have more, someone else must have less.

**Seva (Sanskrit: string):** in Sikhism, volunteer work Selfless service; work offered to God, performed without attachment and with the attitude that one is not the doer. In Siddha Yoga ashrams, Guruseva is a spiritual practice, and students seek to perform all of their tasks in this spirit of selfless offering, Seva is a cornerstone of the Sikh Religion.

**Specificity**: The quality of being specific rather than general.

**Stepford** (as in ***Stepford Wives***): Refers to a movie where all of the wives in a small town act, look and talk just the same in a way that satisfies their husbands' egos.

**Symbiotically**: A relationship of mutual benefit or dependence.

**Vicissitudes**: Sudden or unexpected changes or shifts often encountered in one's life, activities, or surroundings.

**Zero-sum**: Of or relating to a situation in which a gain is offset by an equal loss.

## Bibliography & Recommended Books

Abbott, Edwin A. *Flatland: A Romance of Many Dimensions*. New York: Signet Classic, 1984

Adler, Margot. *Drawing Down the Moon*. Boston: Beacon Press, 1979, 1986.

Amen, Daniel. *Making a Good Brain Great: The Amen Clinic Program for Achieving and Sustaining Optimal Mental Performance*. New York, Harmony Books, 2005.

Ardagh, Arjuna Nick. *Relaxing into Clear Seeing*. Grass Valley: Self X Press, 1998.

Armstrong, Thomas. *7 Kinds of Smart: Identifying and Developing Your Many Intelligences*. New York: Penguin Books, 1993.

Bach, Richard. *Illusions: The Adventures of a Reluctant Messiah*. New York: Dell Publishing, 1977.

Bach, Richard. *The Bridge Across Forever: A Love Story*. New York: Dell Publishing, 1984.

Bach, Richard. *One*. New York: Dell Publishing, 1988.

Bach, Richard. *Running from Safety*. New York: Delta Publishing, 1994.

Bartholomew. *I Come as a Brother*. Carlsbad: Hay House, 1985, 1997.

Bartholomew. *From the Heart of a Gentle Brother*. Carlsbad: Hay House, 1987, 1998.

Bateson, Gregory. *Mind and Nature*. New York: Bantam Books, 1979.

Beattie, Melody. *Codependent No More*. New York: HarperCollins, 1987.

Beyondananda, Swami. *Driving Your Own Karma*. Rochester: Destiny Books, 1989.

Bly, Robert. *Iron John: A Book About Men*. New York, Vintage, 1992.

Brandon, Nathaniel. *The Art of Living Consciously*. New York: Fireside, 1997.

Brewer, Gene. *K-Pax*. New York: St. Martin's Press, 1995. See also the excellent 2001 movie, also called *K-Pax*.

Brewer, Gene. *On a Beam of Light*. New York: St. Martin's Press, 2001.

Brewer, Gene. *K-Pax III: The Worlds of Prot*. London: Bloomsbury Publishing PLC, 2002.

Buscaglia, Leo. *Loving Each Other*. New York: Ballantine Books, 1984.

Capra, Fritjof. *The Tao of Physics*. Boston: Shambala, 1975.

Carey, Ken. *Return of the Bird Tribes*. New York: HarperCollins, 1988.

Carlson, Richard. *Don't Sweat the Small Stuff… and It's all Small Stuff.* New York, Hyperion, 1997.

Carroll, Sean B. *Endless Forms Most Beautiful: The New Science of Evo Devo*. New York: W. W. Norton & Company, 2005.

Castaneda, Carlos. *The Teachings of Don Juan: A Yaqui Way of Knowledge*. New York: Pocket Books, 1968.

Chopra, Deepak. *Quantum Healing: Exploring the Frontiers of Mind/Body Medicine*. New York: Bantam Books, 1990.

Chopra, Deepak. *Ageless Body, Timeless Mind*. New York: Harmony Books, 1993.

Chopra, Deepak. *The Path to Love: Renewing the Power of Spirit in Your Life*. New York: Harmony Books, 1996.

Cohen, Alan. *Dare to be Yourself.* New York: Ballantine Books, 1991.

Cohen, Alan. *I Had It All the Time*. Haiku: Alan Cohen Publications, 1995.

Dalai Lama and Cutler, Howard C. *The Art of Happiness*. New York: Riverhead Books, 1998.

Dass, Ram. *Be Here Now*. New York: Crown Publishing Group, 1971.

Dass, Ram. *The Only Dance There Is*. New York: Anchor Books, 1974.

Dass, Ram. *Grist for the Mill*. Berkeley: Celestial Arts, 1988.

Dass, Ram. *Still Here*. New York: Riverhead Books, 2000.

Dyer, Wayne. *You'll See It When You Believe It*. New York: HarperCollins, 1989.

Dyer, Wayne. *Real Magic*. New York: HarperTorch, 1993.

Dyer, Wayne. *Pulling Your Own Strings*. New York: HarperTorch, 1994.

Ford, Debbie. *The Dark Side of the Light Chasers*. New York: Riverhead Books, 1998.

Ford, Debbie. *The Secret of the Shadow: Owning Your Whole Story*. New York: HarperSanFrancisco, 2002.

Frankl, Viktor. *Man's Search for Meaning*. Boston: Beacon Press, 1959.

Gardner, Barbara. *The Sai Prophecy*. Deerfield Beach: Health Communications, 1999.

Gershenfeld, Neil. *FAB: The Coming Revolution on Your Desktop – From Personal Computers to Personal Fabricators*. New York: Basic Books, 2005.

Gibbs, Jeanne. *Tribes: A New Way of Learning and Being Together*. Windsor, CenterSource Systems, 2001.

Goleman, Daniel. *Emotional Intelligence*. New York: Bantam Books, 1995.

Gordon, Marilyn. *Extraordinary Healing: Transforming Your Consciousness, Your Energy System, and Your Life*. Oakland: WiseWord Publishing, Inc., 2000.

Hanh, Thich Nhat. *Being Peace*. Berkeley: Parallax Press, 1987.

Hanh, Thich Nhat. *Living Buddha, Living Christ*. New York: Riverhead Books, 1995.

Hanh, Thich Nhat. *The Long Road Turns to Joy: A Guide to Walking Meditation*. Berkeley: Parallax Press, 1996.

Hanh, Thich Nhat. *Teachings on Love*. Berkeley: Parallax Press, 1998.

Hanh, Thich Nhat. *The Miracle of Mindfulness*. Boston: Beacon Press, 1999.

Hanh, Thich Nhat. *Anger: Wisdom for Cooling the Flames*. New York: Riverhead Books, 2001.

Hanh, Thich Nhat. *Be Free Where You Are*. Berkeley: Parallax Press, 2002.

Hawken, Paul, Lovins, Amory and Lovins, L. Hunter. *Natural Capitalism*. Boston: Little, Brown and Company, 1999.

Hay, Louise L. *You Can Heal Your Life*. Carlsbad: Hay House, 1984, 1987.

Hendricks, Kathlyn & Hendricks, Gay. *Conscious Loving*. New York: Bantam Books, 1990.

Hendricks, Kathlyn & Hendricks, Gay. *The Conscious Heart*. New York: Bantam Books, 1997.

Hendricks, Gay. *Conscious Living*. New York: HarperSanFrancisco, 2001.

Holmes, Ernest. *The Science of Mind*. New York: G.P. Putnam's Sons, 1997.

Jampolsky, Gerald G. *Love is Letting Go of Fear*. Berkeley: Celestial Arts, 1979.

Johnson, Robert A. *Ecstasy: Understanding the Psychology of Joy*. New York: HarperCollins, 1987.

Johnson, Robert A. *Inner Work*. New York: HarperSanFrancisco, 1989.

Johnson, Robert A. *Owning Your Own Shadow*. New York: HarperCollins, 1991.

Kaufman, Barry Neil. *Happiness is a Choice*. New York: Ballantine Books, 1991.

Keen, Sam. *Fire in the Belly: On Being a Man*. New York: Bantam Books, 1991.

Keyes, Ken, Jr. *Handbook to Higher Consciousness*. Love Line Books, 1975.

Kornfield, Jack. *After the Ecstasy, the Laundry*. New York: Bantam Books, 2000.

Laughlin, Robert B. *A Different Universe: Reinventing Physics from the Bottom Down*. Cambridge: Basic Books, 2005.

Lilly, John. *Center of the Cyclone*. New York: Three Rivers Press, 1985.

Lovelock, James. *Gaia: A New Look at Life on Earth*. Oxford: Oxford University Press, 1979.

McGaa, Ed. *Mother Earth Spirituality*. New York: HarperCollins, 1990.

Millman, Dan. *The Way of the Peaceful Warrior*. Novato: H. J. Kramer Inc., 1980.

Millman, Dan. *No Ordinary Moments: A Peaceful Warrior's Guide to Daily Life*. Novato: H. J. Kramer Inc., 1992.

Nelson, Jane, Lott, Lynn and Glenn, Stephen H. *Positive Discipline A-Z*. Roseville: Prima Publishing, 1999.

Paul, Jordan and Margaret. *Do I Have to Give up Me to be Loved by You?* Minneapolis: CompCare Publishers, 1983.

Pierrakos, Eva & Thesenga, Donovan. *Fear No Evil*. Charlottesville: Pathwork Press, 1993.

Quinn, Daniel. *Ishmael*. New York: Bantam Books, 1995.

Quinn, Daniel. *My Ishmael*. New York: Bantam Books, 1998.

Redfield, James. *Celestine Prophecy*. New York: Warner Books, 1993.

Reich Wilheim. *The Mass Psychology of Fascism*. New York: Farrar, Strauss & Giroux, 1980.

Rengel, Peter. *Living Life in Love*. Larkspur: Imagine Publications, 1995.

Robbins, Ocean and Solomon, Sol. *Choices for our Future: A Generation Rising for Life on Earth*. Summertown: The Book Publishing Company, 1994.

Roberts, Jane. *The Nature of Personal Reality: Specific, Practical Techniques for Solving Everyday Problems and Enriching the Life You Know (A Seth Book)*. San Rafael: Amber-Allen Publishing, 1994.

Rodegast, Pat & Stanton, Judith. *Emmanuel's Book: A Manual for Living Comfortably in the Cosmos*. New York: Bantam Books, 1985.

Roman, Sanaya & Packer, Duane. *Opening to Channel.* Tiburon: H J Kramer Inc., 1987.

Rosenberg, Marshall B. *Non-Violent Communication: A Language of Life*. Encinitas: PuddleDancer Press, 1999.

Russell, Peter. *The While Hole in Time*. New York: HarperCollins, 1992.

Stewart, Katrine. *A Book of Life: Spiritual Journaling in the Twenty-First Century*. Bolivar: Quiet Waters Publications, 2000.

Talbot, Michael. *The Holographic Universe*. New York: HarperCollins, 1991.

Thesenga, Susan & Pierrakos, Eva. *The Undefended Self: Living the Pathwork*. Charlottesville: Pathwork Press, 2001.

Tolle, Eckhart. *The Power of Now*. Novato: New World Library, 1999.

Twist, Lynne. *The Soul of Money: Transforming Your Relationship with Money and Life*. New York: W. W. Norton & Company, 2003.

Twyman, James. *Emissary of Light*. New York: Warner Books, 1998.

Starhawk. *The Fifth Sacred Thing*. New York: Bantam Books, 1993.

Starhawk. *Walking to Mercury*. New York: Bantam Books, 1997.

Veronda. Ronald. *No More Turning Away*. Self-published, 2001.

Walsch, Neale Donald. *Conversations with God: An Uncommon Dialogue (Book 1)*. New York: Putnam Publishing Group, 1996.

Walsch, Neale Donald. *Conversations with God: An Uncommon Dialogue (Book 2)*. Charlottesville: Hampton Roads Publishing Company, 1997.

Wesselman, Hank. *Spiritwalker*. New York: Bantam Books, 1995.

Wesselman, Hank. *Medicinemaker*. New York: Bantam Books, 1998.

Wesselman, Hank. *Visionseeker*. Carlsbad: Hay House, 2001.

Wilber, Ken. *A Brief History of Everything*. Boston: Shambala, 2001.

Williamson, Marianne. *A Return to Love*. New York: HarperCollins, 1992.

Wolf, Fred Alan. *Parallel Universes*. New York: Touchstone, 1988.

Yogananda, Paramahansa. *Autobiography of a Yogi*. Los Angeles: Self-Realization Fellowship Publishers, 1979.

Zukav, Gary. *The Dancing Wu Li Masters*. New York: Bantam, 1980.

Zukav, Gary. *The Seat of the Soul*. New York: Fireside, 1990.

# PERIDOCALS

*BusinessWeek*
*National Geographic*
*Newsweek*
*Popular Science*
*Science & Theology News*
*Shift*
*Smithsonian*
*Spirituality & Health*
*What is Enlightenment?*
*Wired*

## Music for those on the Path...

**Bruce BecVar**: www.shiningstar.com – Exquisite, heart-opening, utterly sublime acoustic guitar.

**Erik Berglund**: www.erikberglund.com – Plays Irish harp and sings like an angel!

**BODHI**: www.shamanicflute.com – Shamanic soundscapes for the journey.

**Krishna Das:** www.triloka.com – Krishna Das has been chanting kirtan on a regular basis in yoga centers all over the world. He has taught with Ram Dass and sung for many saints and yogis here and in India. His chanting is transcendent. All of his CDs are enormously heart-opening.

**Robert Frey**: Singer/songwriter/guitar player/Tantra teacher and workshop leader – Inspiration and heart! Though he has passed on, his love lives in us still. His *Opening to Love* CD is a timeless treasure, and can be ordered at http://www.sacredtantra.com/html/index2.html.

**Kirtana**: www.kirtana.com - Singer/songwriter/guitar player… a huge heart with truly magical music!

**Michael Mandrell**: www.michaelmandrell.com – Lyrical, delightfully original guitar.

**Anton Mizerak:** www.shastasong.com – Essential music for the New Age. Tabla, harmonica, synthesizers and piano.

**Daniel Paul:** www.soundings.com/artists.asp?rd=detail&aid=7 – Outrageous Tabla player, composer and generous heart.

**Soundings of the Planet:** www.soundings.com – artist-owned label. Their motto, "Peace Through Music," says it all.

**Sequoia Records:** www.sequoiarecords.com – Outstanding selection of music, "Designed to balance your life."

**Kathy Zavada:** www.kathyzavada.com – Singer/songwriter/ keyboards sent straight from heaven to our hearts!

# Some Organizations Making a Difference in the World:

**Amnesty International:** www.amnesty.org – Amnesty International (AI) is a worldwide movement of people who campaign for internationally recognized human rights.

AI's vision is of a world in which every person enjoys all of the human rights enshrined in the Universal Declaration of Human Rights and other international human rights standards.

In pursuit of this vision, AI's mission is to undertake research and action focused on preventing and ending grave abuses of the rights to physical and mental integrity, freedom of conscience and expression, and freedom from discrimination, within the context of its work to promote all human rights.

**Be the Change:** http://www.challengeday.org/bethechange/btchome.html – A Challenge Day website, **Be The Change** is a movement inspired by the words and actions of Mohandas (Mahatma) K. Gandhi, and fueled by the vision of what is possible in this world. It consists of like-minded individuals linked by a common desire to make a positive change in the world around them.

**Challenge Day:** www.challengeday.org – Challenge Day's vision is that every child lives in a world where they each feel safe, loved and celebrated.

Challenge Day provides youth and their communities with experiential workshops and programs that demonstrate the possibility of love and connection through the celebration of diversity, truth and full expression.

**Debbie Ford (Ford Institute for Integrative Coaching)**: www.debbieford.com – Debbie Ford, New York Times #1 best-selling author, creator of The Shadow Process, and founder of the Ford Institute for Integrative Coaching, has committed her life to supporting others in leading fully integrated lives.

Debbie Ford is an internationally recognized expert in the field of personal transformation whose books have been translated into twenty-two languages and used as teaching tools in universities and other institutions of learning and enlightenment worldwide.

**The Earth Charter Initiative**: www.earthcharter.org – is the collective name for the extraordinarily diverse, global network of people, organizations, and institutions who participate in promoting the Earth Charter, and in implementing its principles in practice.

The Initiative is a broad-based, voluntary, civil society effort, but participants include leading international institutions, national government agencies, university associations, NGOs, cities, faith groups, and many well-known leaders in sustainable development.

The mission of the Earth Charter Initiative is, "To establish a sound ethical foundation for the emerging global society and to help build a sustainable world based on respect for nature, diversity, universal human rights, economic justice and a culture of peace."

**Foundation for Global Community:** www.globalcommunity.org – The Foundation for Global Community is a nonprofit educational organization, dedicated to reconnecting people, the planet, and prosperity. Recognizing that natural, social, and economic systems are all parts of a single interconnected whole, the Foundation has been promoting cultural change, facilitating personal development, and strengthening community connections for over 50 years.

**Human Awareness Institute**: www.hai.org – The Human Awareness Institute (HAI) produces workshops and other activities related to improving communication and relationships. Dr. Stan Dale originated and led his first workshop in Chicago in 1968. Since then, over 75,000 people have attended HAI's workshops. HAI has grown from a very small family business and one workshop into a series of many workshops led by a highly trained team of facilitators (leaders).

**Institute of Noetic Sciences**: www.ions.org – Exploring the frontiers of consciousness to advance individual, social, and global transformation is the work of the Institute of Noetic Sciences.

The word "noetic" comes from the ancient Greek nous, for which there is no exact equivalent in English. It refers to "inner knowing," a kind of intuitive consciousness – direct and immediate access to knowledge beyond what is available to our normal senses and the power of reason.

Noetic sciences are explorations into the nature and potentials of consciousness using multiple ways of knowing – including intuition, feeling, reason, and the senses. Noetic sciences explore the "inner cosmos" of the mind (consciousness, soul, spirit) and how it relates to the "outer cosmos" of the physical world.

They are a nonprofit membership organization located in Northern California that conducts and sponsors leading-edge research into the potentials and powers of consciousness – including perceptions, beliefs, attention, intention, and intuition.

The institute explores phenomena that do not necessarily fit conventional scientific models, while maintaining a commitment to scientific rigor. The institute is not a spiritual association, political-action group, or a single-cause institute. Rather, it honors open-minded approaches and multiple ways of knowing, bringing discernment while supporting a diversity of perspectives on social and scientific matters.

**Native American Rights Fund**: www.narf.org – Founded in 1970, the Native American Rights Fund (NARF) is the oldest and largest nonprofit law firm dedicated to asserting and defending the rights of Indian tribes, organizations and individuals nationwide.

NARF's practice is concentrated in five key areas: the preservation of tribal existence; the protection of tribal natural resources; the promotion of Native American human rights; the accountability of governments to Native Americans; and the development of Indian law and educating the public about Indian rights, laws, and issues.

**Nature Conservancy**: www.nature.org – The Nature Conservancy is a leading international, nonprofit organization dedicated to preserving the diversity of life on Earth. The mission of The Nature Conservancy is to preserve the plants, animals and natural communities that represent the diversity of life on Earth by protecting the lands and waters they need to survive.

**One World Children's Fund**: www.owcf.org – The One World Children's Fund mission is to network aid directly to grassroots organizations that support disadvantaged children from around the world. They recognize that local people know best how to resolve problems in their communities when they have access to resources to build a sustainable future for children and their families.

One World Children's Fund envisions a world where all children have rights to basic education and human dignity. OWCF links donors in the USA with innovative grassroots organizations globally. The focus of outreach includes basic needs, education, and women's empowerment.

**Shift *in action***: http://www.shiftinaction.com/ – An Institute of Noetic Sciences Website.

**Spiritual Cinema Circle**: www.spiritualcinemacircle.com – When you join The Spiritual Cinema Circle you will be making an important contribution to your world. By joining The Circle, you will bring inspiring and enlightening entertainment into your own life while positively influencing the lives of others.

Through your support, you are encouraging talented, visionary filmmakers to continue in their efforts to add life and meaning to our movies. For years now, these filmmakers have been over looked by mainstream distributors looking for big profits. As a result we have all experienced the spread of movies that glorify violence and foster negative stereotypes in our culture's mindset, ultimately leading to a general emotional and spiritual numbness.

By joining in this movement for quality entertainment, you will also be taking steps to raise the consciousness of the world today by supporting and experiencing truly nourishing entertainment. It is time for us all to own and use our power to create the world of our dreams!

**Transformational Book Circle:** www.transformationalbookcircle.com The world's first transformational reading community. By joining together, you can create powerful changes in your own life, and at the same time make a genuine contribution to a more harmonious world.

# Index

## A

## B

**D**

## E

**H**

## I

## J



## K



## L

**Q**



**R**

## S

## T

# Notes

# Notes

# Notes

# About the author:

Steve Ryals lives with his beloved wife JoAnn in the wild mountains of Mendocino County in Northern California. They thrive in an off-the-grid environment, producing most of their electricity from solar panels, with hydro in the winter. *Drunk with Wonder* was written, edited and designed with almost no help from fossil fuels.

This book is printed on 60# Thor Offset acid-free, recycled paper (85% recovered fiber, 30% post consumer). Please be kind to the environment and recycle!

On a clear day they can see a strip of the Pacific Ocean, about 20 air miles to the West. Happier than they've ever been in their lives, Steve and JoAnn take the time *every single day* to feel grateful for their many Blessings.

A study guide for *Drunk with Wonder* is in the works. Please see www.rockcreekpress.com or www.drunkwithwonder.com for more details.

# Drunk with Wonder
## BOOK ORDER FORM

🖷 Fax orders: 419.589.4040. Please include a copy of this form.

☎ Phone orders: Call toll free 888.247.6553 and have your credit card ready.

💻 Email orders: order@bookmasters.com.

✉ Mail orders: Rock Creek Press, 30 Amberwood Parkway, Ashland, Oh. 44805.

Please send ______ copies of Drunk with Wonder (at $17.95 each) to:

Full Name: ____________________________________________

Company or Organization: ______________________________
(If relevant)

Shipping Address: ____________________________________________

City ______________________ State ______ Zip ____________

Phone: ______________________ Email: ______________________
(In case we have questions about your order) (Your email will never be sold or given away)

Name on Card ____________________________________________

Billing Address ____________________________________________
(If different from mailing address)

City ______________________ State ______ Zip ____________

Please charge my: ❑ Visa ❑ MC ❑ AMEX ❑ Discover $ ____________

Card # ______________________________ Exp. Date ____________

Signature as it appears on Card ______________________________

❑ Check Enclosed for $ ____________ (Payable to **Rock Creek Press**)
(Please allow 3-4 weeks if paying by check)

**Please add $6.00** for shipping for **EACH** book ordered. All books are shipped by Priority Mail.

**Sales Tax:** Please add 7.75% sales tax for orders shipped to California addresses.
Please add 7.00% sales tax for orders shipped to Ohio addresses.

To subscribe to our *Drunk with Wonder* email newsletter, visit www.drunkwithwonder.com and sign up.